WALT KELLY'S
POGO
Romances
Recaptured

containing the complete volumes of

POGO: PRISONER OF LOVE
THE INCOMPLEAT POGO

A Fireside Book
Simon and Schuster

SBN 671-22184-1
MANUFACTURED IN THE UNITED STATES OF AMERICA
1 2 3 4 5 6 7 8 9 10

CONTENTS

POGO: PRISONER OF LOVE

THE INCOMPLEAT POGO

POGO: PRISONER OF LOVE

POGO:
PRISONER OF LOVE

THIS BOOK IS

for ANNA
WAGONNY
CAMERANO

with love...

THE GOOD OLD
OLDTIME
NEW START

One of the happy accidents of being a cartoonist is the discovery, practically by chance, that people are dependable and steadfast. We can be relied upon for the gold of comic material which also can pan out to be the fool's gold of tragedy. Despite the fact that we repeat our acts of boobism over and over, we are always surprising and fascinating. There is a kind of hypnotism in watching our wriggling mirror reflections.

In these times, the word "student" or the word "cop" can scarcely be uttered by most except as an epithet. We have had constant revolution since the year One because we like to start anew, our way. Having fouled up one home, we leave our litter behind to write a brave new constitution in a land far off and considerably upwind from the dump.

But now, through lack of space, we have to face each other in the dark and uneasy environs of the familiar. So it occurs to the cartoonist that the easiest war is the one in the home where railing males and females, family bound, can relieve the tedium with the age-old fight of love.

CHAPTER 1

THE TRUEST LIE
IS YOUTH REMEMBERED

12

SOME EARLY THREAT
OF PROMISE

WHAT WE SHOULD DO IS E·LECT A *NEW* GROUN'HOG... *EVEN I* CAN OUT-**GROUN'HOG** OL' GRUNDOON.

2-6

WHAT'S THE JOB AMOUNT TO? *SLEEPIN'!* ANYBODY CAN DO IT. GRUNDOON JUS' *SLOBBED* OUT. *HE* NEEDS A *GOOD* TALK! TIME IS A-WASTIN'....

I'LL GO SEE HIM *POST-HASTE!* *TOOT SWEET!* SHAKE HIM *UP!* SHOW HIM US A-DULTS GITS AT THINGS RIGHT AWAY. *SNAP! SNAP!* *1-2-3! GIT GOIN'!*

♪

RIGHT AFTER SUPPER.

ALL THIS TALK OF YOURS ABOUT *E·LECTIN'* A *NEW* GROUN'HOG 'CAUSE TH' OLD ONE DIN'T LET US KNOW WHEN *SPRING'S* COMIN'...
...COULD *YOU* DO BETTER'N *HIM?*

HO!

2-7

AT LEAS' AS A GROUN'HOG *I'D* GIT OUT THERE AN' *I'D WORK*... I'D *IMMEDIATE* GO TO SLEEP... I'D DO *MY* DUTY RIGHT A-WAY.

AN' YOU'D WAKE UP?

ON TIME?

IS THEY ANYMORE PIE?

LOOK! HERE I AM BEIN' A LI'L' GROUN'HOG ... I'M SLEEPIN' ... BUT I FEEL SPRING IN MY BONES.

2-8

I SNORE ON THRU THE LUMPS OF LAST DAYS OF WINTER ...

HEY, OL' PORKYPINE HAVE SOME PIE ...

THEN I'D GRACE-FOOLY A-WAKEN AND ...

PIE'S GOOD FOR YOU ... CLEANS UP WARTS AN' ALL.

IT'S MY FAVOR-ITE VITAMIN

.. AND I WOULD ... ... MM ... IS THEY ANYMORE PIE ... ?

CHAPTER 3

WARPATH TO PEACE

DEACON! I AND ALBERT GOT A *GREAT* IDEA!

?

WE'RE GONNA *SEE-CEDE!*

My great great Gran'pa tried it once --- But Gran'ma caught him at the border with the Sunday collection.

All $1.39½ of it.

OH, WE AIN'T TRYIN' NO *PETTY LARCENARY* STUFF.... *WE* ARE STARTIN' A *BRAN' NEW COUNTRY*.... RIGHT, ALBERT?

YOU LOST MY *SEE-GAR!*

LIKE THE KID HERE SAYS, IF WE STARTS A NEW COUNTRY, *HE'LL* GET TO BE THE *SECRETARY OF GROUN'HOGGISM* AN' *I'LL* BE THE *SECRETARY* OF *EDUCATION!*

2-18

Din't know that either of you was a expert in them fields!

NATURALLY! I, FOR INSTINCE, WOULD **OPEN** THE KIDS' **MINDS** TO EDUCATION....

How?

THE WAY THEIR MINDS IS WORKIN' I'D TRY OPENIN' 'EM WITH A DOSE FROM **OLD DOCTOR TWELVE GAUGE** HERE, RIGHT, ALBERT?

If you want to be Secretary of Education, **Wiley Catt**, let's have a run-down of your schooling.

NATCH.... IT WON'T TAKE A SECOND....

FIGGERS.

2-19

WENT THIRTEEN YEARS STRAIGHT TO SCHOOL LEARNIN' **BASICS.**

THEN....UM **THEN**....

Yes? Yes?

I QUIT.

You **DROPPED OUT**?

ME?! A **DROP-OUT**!?! SIR, THAT IS A **SLUR**! A **UNPATRIOCKIWOCKLE INSULT**! I DIN'T DROP OUT! I JUS' PLAIN **QUIT**!

23

Why'd you quit school after 13 years?

'CAUSE I WAS **STIFF.**

GOOD BOY!

2-20

DURIN' **MY HALCYONIAN** DAYS, WE USETA MAKE THE STUFF DOWN IN THE FURNACE ROOM 'TIL A LEAK DEVELOPED AN' **EVERYBODY** WAS A **DROP-OUT**---ACTUAL A BLOW-OUT---

I DON'T MEAN **THAT**--- I WAS STIFF FROM **SETTIN'**----

HOW DULL----

YEP---MAYBE YOU'VE **NOTICED**--- STUFFIN' YERSELF INTO THEM **SECOND GRADE CHAIRS** WHEN YOU'RE GOIN' ON **TWENTY YEAR OLD** KIN BE AWFUL TRYIN'---

What else qualifies you to be **Secretary of Education?**

CHURCHY TAUGHT ME TO **READ.**

2-21

I LEARNT HOW TO READ **HALF** OF **POGO'S** NAME ---- I'M A EXPERT ON THE "O" PART--- LISTEN---- O, O, O, O, O --- GREAT, HUH?

"O" is the same thing as **ZERO?**

24

AND ZERO IS NOTHIN'?

Well, if you're good at reading the infinite zero~~~~

~~~~perchance you'd make a great Secretary of the Treasury~~~

WHY NOT?

As prospective secretaries in the country to be formed, we'll join the Pure, the Brave, the Wise and the Innocent~~~ Come! We'll go see the respected Molester Mole!

2-24

OL' MOLE?

MAN, HE AIN'T INNOCENT OF ANYTHING~~~

27

THE IMPOSSIBLE POSSIBLED

3-1

3-3

29

31

3-7

CHAPTER 5

AN ANTHEM OF NOTE (ONE)

AND THEN *I*... *HEY!*

SEE! SEE WHAT WE HAVE HERE IN THE DOG? THE NEW SECRETARY OF *PROBLEMS!*

?

3-11

WE HAVE *YOU,* WITH A *FIRM GRASP* OF *NOTHING OR ZERO,* AS SECRETARY OF TREASURY AND/OR EDUCATION···· *ALBERT,* WHO CAN'T TALK, *SECRETARY OF STATE* ···· ·····*THEN*··· *BEAUREGARD.*

HAR! PUT OL' DOG IN CHARGE OF *PROBLEMS* AND YOU'LL HAVE ONES NOBODY HEARD OF···· HE HAD TO SEND OFF FOR A *CORRESPONDENCE COURSE* ON HOW TO TIE HIS SHOES····

EXACTLY! THE PUBLIC IS TIRED OF *OLD PROBLEMS*····WE NEED *NEW, VIBRANT,* FASCINATING PROBLEMS···· *BEAUREGARD'S BRAIN* WILL SUPPLY THEM, CORRECT?

HERE'S THE KEY TO OUR WHOLE SCHEME FOR *SECESSION*····

♪

3-15

WE, AS A CABINET, NEED A *PRESIDENT.*

SO, YOU GOT YER **VOICE BACK**? DOIN' ANY MORE **SINGIN'**?

ONLY THE ANTHEM OUR **SECESSIONIST** TEAM IS ENDORSED ...IT'S ALL **ONE** NOTE.

3-19

EVERY ONE OF WHICH I CAN PERSON'LY **HIT** ♪ "OH, I WAS EATIN' SOME **CHOP SUEY** WITH A **LADY** ♪♪ IN **SAINT LOOIE**...." ♪

IT DON'T GOT MUCH **UP-LIFT**.

NOR **DOWN**-LIFT EITHER... IT'S **DIRECT**....GOT NO TIME FOR DETOURS **UP** OR **DOWN** ...

WAY THINGS ARE THESE DAYS A COUNTRY GOTTA RUN **STRAIGHT** AN' **FAST** JUST TO STAY IN ONE PLACE.

JUST 'CAUSE YOU CAN'T SING THE CURRENT **NATIONABLE** ANTHEM AIN'T REASON ENOUGH TO **SECEDE**.

'TAIN'T THE **ONLY** REASON... TAKE OL' **GRUNDOON**...

3-20

THAT GROUN'HOG WAS S'POSE TO **WAKE UP** AN' TELL US WHEN **SPRING** WAS COMIN'! DID HE? **NO!** CALL THAT **FEDERABOBBLE RESPONSIBILLY**?

CHAPTER 6

THE SOMNAMBULISTIC MISSILE

JOB GOT ONE DRAWBACK....

THINKIN' UP A *REAL* BRAN' NEW PROBLEM IS A *REAL* PROBLEM.

BEAUREGARD, YOU SAY MOLE WANTS YOU TO BE SECRETARY OF *PROBLEMS*?

YEP.... A *TOUGH JOB.*

3-27

THERE'S THE GUY TO HELP YOU... CHURCHY... HE'S A VERTIWOCKLE *EX*-PERT ON PROBLEMS.

BUT *MY* PROBLEM IS *NEW* PROBLEMS... Y'KNOW, *THINKIN'* EM UP.

THEN CHURCHY IS YOUR MAN.....TO *HIM,* ALL PROBLEMS IS *NEW.*

Z

OKAY.... YOU CAN TALK TO HIM *NOW*, BEAUREGARD....

Z

WHAT'S GOIN' ON?

BEAUREGARD WANTED TO TALK TO CHURCHY... BUT OL' HOUN' DOG FELL ASLEEP WAITIN'...

3-31

EASILY FIXED.... *WAKE UP!*

ALBERT, YOU LOST YOUR VOICE AGAIN *AND* DIN'T WAKE THE DOG *AND* KNOCKED OUT *CHURCHY* AGAIN.

OONK... GUNK GORP...

CHAPTER 7

BRAIN TRUST BUST

WHAT DO YOU THINK OF THE **OKEFENOKEE** SECEDIN' FROM THE **U.S. AND A.**, SAM?

SECESSION IS **ALWAYS** GOOD...ALL ACCORDIN' TO **WHAT** HUNK TAKES OFF...

I'D SUGGEST WE SECEDE WITH A **DIFFER'NT PATCH** OF GROUND CENTERIN' AROUND OUR **HEART** LAND.

4-7

HEART LAND? **WASHINGTON, D.C.?**

FORT KNOX.

SUPPOSE OUR NEW COUNTRY **DID** MAKE OFF WITH **FORT KNOX**...? ...**FIRST** THINGS BEING FIRST?

FIRST THINGS BEIN' **FIRST**?

4-8

WE WOULDN'T PAY **NO TAXES**....

GRAND!

WE'D FEED THE **STARVING**.

?

46

47

48

YOU BOYS **GO** TO THE FORT AND **POKE** AROUND.... THEN REPORT BACK.

POKE IT IS!

NOW! **WHICH** FORT DID HE SAY?

UM.... FORT....**UH**.... HMM....WELL MM·YEH· UM....

HEIGHDY, BEAUREGARD, HOW'S THE **SECRETARY** OF **PROBLEMS** COMIN'?

GOT A BIG PROBLEM WITH OUR **NEW ANTHEM**....

4-12

"OH, STAND UP AND COUNT YOUR NOSES, OUR LAND'S A BED OF ROSES RIGHT FROM YOUR HEAD TO TOE-SES" ....**NOW WHAT NEXT?**

"OUR DOOR WE NEVER CLOSES"....

GREAT! GREAT!

.... AT LEAST IT **RHYMES**.... DON'T **MEAN** MUCH THO!

LONG AS IT **RHYMES**.... WE CAN MAKE IT **MEAN** SOMETHIN' LATER.

CHAPTER 8

A SECRET: SWIFT, SHORT, SWEET, AND DEAD

A FORT OF ONE SYLLABLE? *NATURALLY, FORT MUDGE!*

YOU GOT IT!

4-15

GIVE THAT **HYPOTHESIS** A QUICK **TRUTH TEST!** SEE IF OUR **OCCULT** BRAINS IS ON THE WIRE--- TWO DROPS OF **BANEWORT** IN THE **GRUMION**....

BLORP!

AFFIRMATIVE!

ANOTHER *FIRST!*

NOW, DISGUISED AS SIMPLE **ARCHAEOLOGISTS** WE'LL SNOOP AROUND ON OUR **SECRET** MISSION.

TO EXPLORE **FORT MUDGE** FOR OUR **NEW GUMMINT.**

HEY!

4-16

SHH----WE'S ON A **SECRET MISSION** FOR THE **GUMMINT**--- *DON'T TELL NOBODY.*

DAD BURN!

51

4-17

CHAPTER 9

A MUFFLED MISS MUFFET

CHAPTER 10

ERGO EGO

56

AND WHEN THE **QUISLING YAPPED** ON EVERY SIDE, **WHO** SAID "YE SHALL NOT PASS!"? **WHO** GAVE HIS **ALL**? **WHO**?

YEAH, **WHO!**

ME! THE **NOBLE** DOG! MAN'S **BEST FRIEND!** A-LERT, A-WARE! NOW **CAST** ASIDE! **ABANDONED! GULP** ...A PIECE OF **FLOTSAM** AND **JELLY-SAM** (...**SNIFF**...)

THERE THERE... **BLOW**

SUCH A **SORRY** WAY TO TREAT MAN'S BEST FRIEND... **THROWIN' ALL DOGS OUT OF THE ANTHEM** ...HOO... GULP

?

YOU JUST REST... I'LL WHOP UP SOMETHIN' TO CALM YOU DOWN.

4-26

WHAT'S WRONG, BEAUREGARD?

I'M **CAST** ASIDE! DOWN-SPURNED BY HITHERTO BOSOM BUDDIES! MAN'S BEST FRIEND, IS BEEN CRUELLY GIVE THE **BACK OF THE BRUSH!**

WHO DID THIS TO YOU, **OLD FRIEND**...? I'LL START A **PROGRAM** OF **TEARIN' HIM** LIMB FROM LIMB!

HIM

HIM? **HUM!** MM... WELL, WHY DON'T WE PUT OFF **MY** PROGRAM 'TIL AFTER LUNCH?

HERE WE ARE.

CHAPTER 11

ENOUGH IS PLENTY

HOW **LOVELY** TO SEE YOU, MIZ GROUN' SQUIRREL.

NEVER MIND THE **BOOBUS-CLABBER!** YOU MENS BETTER GET BUSY! US WOMEN **ALLUS** DOES ALL THE **WAPPUNDANGLE** WORK····YOU SLEEZERY **SLOGGERS** *RUNS OUT!* **NEVER** DOES NOTHIN'!

4-29

THAT'S WHY US GIRLS IS····UM····UH····

HAVE A **CUPPA COCOA** AND A **CRUMB BUN**, MIZ GROUN' SQUIRREL.

YA THROWS US (GLOB) OUT OF YOUR **FANDANGLIN'** NIPSIDED MEETIN'S AN' (GLOMP) YA DON'T GIVE US A **WAGTAILED VOTE**····AND (GOBBLE) (GOOK) **BANG SLANG!**

SUCH **LANGUAGE!**

ANYTHIN' **ELSE,** MIZ GROUN'-SQUIRREL?

(SLURP!) Y'MEAN TALKIN'-WISE OR EATIN'-WISE?

AFTER ALL US GIRLS IS **SACKERFICED!** RAISIN' THE **CHILLUN!** WORKIN' LIKE **SLAVES** IN THE KITCHEN! **CLEANIN' UP** AFTER YOU **MENS!** YOU MENS TREAT US LIKE **DIRT!**

4-30

BUT **YOU** IS A YOUNG **WIDOW WOMAN** OF A FEW SPRINGS AN' SUMMERS AN' NO CHILLUN **ATALL** ·····SO HOW CAN **YOU** GO ON LIKE····

5-1

CHAPTER 12

EASY COME, QUEASY GO

CAPTAIN KIDD, HUH?····WELL MM—UM YES···

HE WAS A **PIRATE**, WASN'T HE?

CAPTAIN KIDD 1697

5-5

Y'MEAN ONE OF THEM AS CUTS YER HEAD OFF WITH A **HARQUEBUS**?

THE **SAME**····· THEN HE MAKES YA WALK THE **PLANK**···

WHY DON'T **YOU** OPEN IT UP AN' SEE IF IT'S **HIM**?

I HAR'LY KNOW HIM····· HE BEEN **GONE** FOR NEARLY **300** YEARS!

CAPTAIN KIDD 1697

I'LL STAND OUT OF THE WAY HERE WHILST YOU PRY THE COVER OFF THE ·UH···UM **OSSUARIUM**·····

I'LL STAND **WITH** YOU····I NEVER DESERTS A OL' PAL IN A TIME LIKE THIS.

ANYTHING HAPPENIN' TO **CAPTAIN KIDD'S SARCOPHAGUS**?

IT'S JUS' **LAYIN'** THERE. NOT SAYIN' A WORD.

5-6

Y'AIN'T AFEARED TO **OPEN** IT, ARE YA?

'COURSE NOT···AN' NEITHER IS **YOU**, I TRUST.

MMPH ☆

63

64

I BE DOUBLE DANGBLOTTED IF I DIN'T FALL ASLEEP ON A *JUNK PILE*.

5-8

PROLLY A *TRICK* OF THEM *WAGGLASTED, PIGSTEEPLED, MEN* ... THEY'S ALLUS *FUNNIN'* IT UP WITH US GIRLS WHAT'S TRYIN' TO KEEP OUR COUNTRY *UNPOLLUTED* ...

I'LL *SHOW 'EM!* I'LL GET *RID* OF THE *CATFLABBIN' LOT!*

IF THEY'S *ANYTHIN'* I HATES IT'S THAT *SLOBBIN' LITTER* AN' THEM *POLLUTIONS* ... GACK!

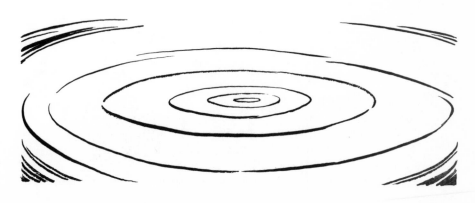

CHAPTER 13

A RANK CASE OF REASON

THIS IS A OL' TRUNK WE FOUND... KEPT TELLIN' DEACON TO TAKE IT T'*YOUR* PLACE, MOLE... FER *SAFE KEEPIN'*.

MY *WORD!*

YOU HAVE DISCOVERED **CAPTAIN KIDD'S** *TREASURE* OF **PEARLS, RUBIES, GOLD,** PLAIN MONEY AND **TRADING STAMPS!**

WE *HAVE?*

THAT'S WHAT I *MEAN*... I'LL TAKE IT TO *MY* *PLACE*... JUST FOR *SAFE KEEPIN'*.

LOOK! MOLE, DEACON AN' WILEY CATT MAKIN' OFF WITH **CAPTAIN KIDD'S** REMAINS.

THAT'S PRACTICALLY *GRAVE ROBBIN'*... US TRUE HEARTED TYPES SHOULN'T *ALLOW* THAT... WE SHOULD TAKE UP ARMS AND **MOUNT AN OFFENSIVE**...

AN OFFENSIVE **WHAT**?

IT'S AT TIMES LIKE THIS THAT THE *REAL NEED* FOR A B.A.M. SYSTEM COMES *ALIVE*...

5-14

DON'T YOU MEAN THE A.B.M. SYSTEM?

NO.... I BELIEVE **BAM** SPELLS IT OUT BETTER...

CHAPTER 14

A BUSTLE OF MUSCLE

I HEAR TELL THE WOMEN IS *ORGANIZIN'*--- THEY CLAIM THEY BEEN **SHORT CHANGED**....

NATCH

5-17

THEY SAYS THEY WANTS **JUSTICE**.

NATCH

BUT THEY IS *ARMIN'* THEIRSELVES....THEY WANT *JUSTICE* BUT AIN'T GOIN' THROUGH *LAW*.

NATCH

SEE, THERE'S THE *LADIES AID* HAVIN' A *PEP RALLY*.

5-19

SHOULD WE *SNEAK UP* AN' FIND OUT WHAT ALL THEY'S *RE-BELLIN' ABOUT* AN' ALL?

INVADE PRIVACY? HAH!

5-20

DANG! RAN RIGHT INTO SOMEBODY'S NEW WASHED CLOTHES.

5-26

HELLO, SISTER! WERE YOU AT THE BIG LADIES AID RALLY WHERE WE HOOTED AN' HOLLERED AN' CARRIED ON? LANDY LAURA MERCY WHAT A DO!

HEH HEH, THAT SO? WELL, WHAT WAS IT ALL ABOUT, MIZZUS?

OH, LAND! WE SCREECHED AN' SPEECHED AN' WROTE THREATENIN' LETTERS.

MIZ BEAVER GOT IN A THREE ROUND DISCUSSION 'BOUT A MOTION; MIZ RABBIT HAD A SET OF THE SWOONS; WE BROKE 19 PLATES...WODDYA MEAN? WHAT WAS IT ALL ABOUT?

YOU SEEM TO BE HAVIN' TROUBLE WITH YER CLOTHES, SIS.

AIN'T MINE. I RUN INTO 'EM KINDA ACCIDENTAL.

5-27

WELL, I'LL BE.... THIS LOOKS LIKE MIZ BEAVER'S YARD... THAT'S HER WASH, I WARRANT.

ORG

WHEN SHE COMES BACK, I WOON'T WANNA BE IN *YOUR* SKIN, MISS, UH--M-- *WHAT IS* YOUR NAME, HON?

ORG!

ORG?...STRANGE MONICKER, SIS....MM, SHORT FOR ORGANDY, I S'POSE.... *HERE* COMES MIZ BEAVER, NOW.

HEIGHDY, MIZ BEAVER, I'D LIKE YOU TO MEET A NEW FRIEND, *MISS ORG.*

OUR LADIES COMMITTEE IS VOTED TO *GIT* TH' *MEN'S PRESIDENT.*

OL' *MOLE* CLAIM *POGO* IS THEIR HEAD MAN.....SO, IF WE CAPTURES *HIM*, ONE OF US *MARRIES* THE CRITTUR.....

5-28

....THUS BECOMIN' THE *FIRST LADY* AN' THUS GITS TO *RUN THE SHOW!*

WELL, WELL, WELL, THAT MIGHT INTEREST MISS ORG, HERE.... MISS ORG? *HEY, ORG!*

CHAPTER 15

OUT WITH THE WASH

Y'SAY THAT'S **CAP'N KIDD'S** *TREASURE*, MOLE?

AYE, WILEY CATT SET ME HERE TO GUARD IT.

GUARD IT? C'MON MAN, LET'S *OPEN IT!*

6-4

THERE'S A CURSE ON THE *FIRST* MAN TO OPEN IT, SAM.

SO... A LITTLE PATIENCE.....

YOU BET... 100 *PER CENT* NOBLESSE *O·BLIGE.* WE'LL WAIT FOR GOOD OL' *WILEY.*

'LONG AS THERE'S A CURSE ON WHO-EVER OPENS THE TRUNK *FIRST*, MOLE', WHY *GUARD* IT? WE'LL LIE IN *AMBUSH* IN THE COMFORTABLE TALL GRASS....

6-5

READY TO VIGILANTLY *POUNCE* UPON THE FIRST UNWARY CULPRIT WHOMSOEVER SNEAKS IN.

VIGILANCE! VIGILANCE!

78

6-6

BUT I DIN'T DO NO SUCH OF A—

STAY! MY FRIEND, ALSO I, YOUR BOSOM CHUM, IS BEEN BAD PUT ON BY FEE-MALES.

WAIT A DAGBONE MINUTE! DID YOU EVER PROMISE A SWEET YOUNG YEMMENITE, NAME OF BUBBLES, ANYTHING? BECAUSE, BY GAR AN' BY SCRUMBAG, SIR, I....

ORG

YOU'RE A PRISONER OF LOVE, POGO... TO ERR IS HUMAN.... AN' YOU'RE AS HUMAN AS THE NEXT, AN' THAT'S GOIN' SOME.... ... LEMME HELP YOU OUTTA THE CLOTHES.

6-11

BEEN TRYIN' TO UNTANGLE 'EM ... CAREFUL NOW, MOUSE.

THEY BELONGS TO MIZ BEAVER... SO BE CAREFUL, SON....

DON'T FRET, I WON'T CUT YOU...

WOULDN'T WANT NO HARM TO COME TO 'EM....

WELL, WHY DIN'T YOU SAY SO, PRISONER OF LOVE, OL' BUDDY?

CHAPTER 16

GACKSCRAGGLE EXPLORED

FIRST CLASS,
SPECIAL DELIVERY FEE-MALE

86

HOO BOY! THERE AIN'T *NO MORE*, IS THERE?

THE *BEST* PART.

♪ A furore for our Nora! And applaud Aurora seen! Where, throughout the summer has our Borealis been? ♫

YA WON'T CATCH *ME* ASKIN' AGAIN.

WE'LL JUST WALK OVER AN' TELL MOLE THAT POGO SHOULD HAVE A *FIRST LADY* IF HE'S PRESIDENT.

AN' A SECOND LADY.... LIKE A VICE-PRES....

6-19

HOW'D THEM MEN PICK OLD *POGO* TO BE THEIR PRESIDENT?

WELL, HE'S HONEST, PURE, TRUTHFUL, COURAGEOUS, KINDLY, NOBLE, *TRUSTING*....

.... AN' *MALLEABLE*.

♪ I may be somewhat dalliable; My love is most infalliable, Utmostly true and malleable! And---- ♫

HEY.... NOT SO *FAST!*

CHAPTER 18

THE WONT OF DON'T

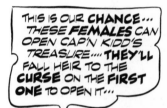

CHAPTER 19

AHEAD IN THE FRIDGE

PARM **ME**....I SAID, "OUR COUNTRY NEEDS A **COOLER HEAD**"....AN' **YOU** SAID, "HOW 'BOUT ALBERT?"

MUNCH....

ALL VERY **TRUE**.

AN' **I** SAID, "**ALBERT**!? A **COOLER HEAD**?"....AN' **YOU** SAID, "SURE, HE KEEPS **HIS** IN THE **ICEBOX**...."

WANNA **SEE**?

6-30

NOT ON A **EMPTY** STOMACH.

HEY.... I MEANT HE....

Who but the noble dog ♫ Took our land thru the bog Thru the fog, thru the smog Who but the daring dog?

THIS ANTHEM AIN'T ABOUT **DOGS**....IT'S ABOUT OUR **COUNTRY**.

HEY!

ME AND PORKY WAS TALKIN' 'BOUT **COOLER HEADS**....AN' PORKY SAYS ALBERT IS GOT THE COOLEST BECAUSE....

7-1

94

AH, YES! A REAL **COOL** ONE.... **HE** WAS THE **FIRST** TO OBJECT TO THE **OLD ANTHEM**... HIS COOL HEAD TOLE HIM IT WAS TOO **HIGH** TO SING.

HIS HEAD IS COOL 'CAUSE HE KEEPS IT IN THE **ICEBOX**.

WELL.... UM-HMM.... ....YOU....

....DON'T MEAN....

EXACTLY!

HE WAS THE **FIRST** TO ADVISE **SECESSION** SO'S WE'D GIT A ANTHEM WE COULD **SING**.

WHAT **GLORY** LAY IN HIS PATH....

SURE ....HE WOULD OF BEEN ONE OF OUR **FUTURE FOREFATHERS**.

GOOD! I'VE FOUND YOU, OWL .... I'M AFRAID YOU'VE **MISUNDERSTOOD** ME, SIR, WHEN I SAID **ALBERT** KEEPS HIS **HEAD** IN THE **ICEBOX**....

YES?

7-3

I MERELY MEANT THAT HE'S GOT HIS HEAD IN THERE TO SAMPLE THIS AN' THAT AN' MUNCH AN'....Y'KNOW?

THAT'S *IT!*

HE TAKES HIS HEAD OFF EVERY NIGHT AN' SETS IT IN THE ICEBOX...

WHERE, *UN-SEEN* AN' *UNKNOWN*, IT EATS AWAY *THRU* THE NIGHT...

ALBERT PUTTIN' HIS HEAD INTO THE ICE-BOX COMES AS A *STAGGERER*...

WE'LL *RELAX* BY GOIN' BACK TO WRITIN' A *NEW ANTHEM*...

7-4

HOW'S *THIS*....

Once born as a infant in a lowly log-cabin was the ever-lovin', blue-eyed dog And~~~

YOUR ANTHEMS IS STILL ALL ABOUT *DOGS*.

IT BEIN' *FOURTH OF JULY* AN' ALL, *I STILL* LIKES THE *OLD* NATIONAL SONG.

I AGREES... WHAT'S *WRONG* WITH *DIXIE?*

96

CHAPTER 20

TWO SHOTS FOR THE ROAD

98

ME, *FAINT?!*....NEVER!

GOOD WORK, POGO....INTO THE BOAT.... STAY UNDER COVER.

WHAT'S GOIN' **ON**, SEMINOLE SAM?!... AIN'T **MOLE** AN' **YOU** GUARDIN' MY **TREASURE CHEST?**

MOLE'S FAINTED, WILEY CATT! AN' THE **TRUNK** IS *AFTER* ME....

7-9

DON'T GET OUT FROM UNDER YET, POGO.... IT MIGHT NOT BE *SAFE.*

MOUSE, IT'S GETTIN' **DARK** AND I HAVE *HAD* THAT OL' TRUNK.

HONEY TIGER THE GOOD SHIP BOOMER

7-10

WHY, THAT AIN'T MY TREASURE CHEST **ALONE**....IT'S A COUPLE **TRUNKNAPPERS** STEALIN' MY PROPERTY!

WILEY, **DON'T SHOOT!** IT MIGHT BE **SOMEBODY** WE DON'T EVEN **KNOW!**

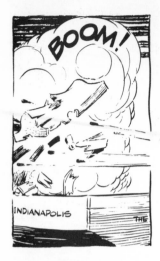

BOOM!

INDIANAPOLIS   THE

I *TOLE* YOU IT WASN'T SAFE, YET, POG'.

WANNA GET BACK IN THE TRUNK?

1959   S.S. HONEY-TIGER

C'MON MOUSE, WE'S DRIFTED ASHORE....LET'S GIT GOIN' WHILE IT'S DARK.

YEH.....I *ALLUS* FEELS SAFER IN THE DARK.

7-11

DARK IS *BEST*.... AFTER A LIFETIME OF HAUNTIN' HOUSES, FIGHTIN' CATS AN' SECOND STORY WORK, I LEARNT *NEVER* WORK IN THE DAY TIME..... A *SOLID RULE!* *SAFE!*

EVERY BODY KNOWS IT?

EVERY BODY...

ACK

COURSE THERE'S *ALLUS* SOME IGNORANT DANG FOOL WHAT AIN'T HEARN OF IT.

100

MOUSE, Y'KNOW WHO FIRED AT US? MISS MA'M'SELLE **HEPZIBAH**···

A DAME!

ONE OF THEM WHAT'S MADE YOU A **PRISONER OF LOVE**?··· WANTS TO **MARRY YOU**?

HECK, NO····

THIS ONE IS A **FRIEND** OF MINE.

IT'S ONLY **US,** MISS MA'M'SELLE···· DON'T SHOOT NO MORE.

POGO! I AM SORRY I AM SHOOT THESE GUN AT YOU, M'SIEUR!

BUT···· YOU WERE NO IN THE **DANGER,** YES? I AM NO GOOD A **MARKSMAN**····N'EST-CE PAS? **NON**?

OH, I DUNNO, MA'M... YOU GOT **CLOSE**... LOOK AT THE **HOLES** IN MY HAT.

MAGNIFIQUE! I AM **IMPROVE!** PERHAP NEXT TIME I... ...BUT **NON**...ALORS... WHAT I AM **SAYING?**

THE **REASON** I AM SHOOT IS BECAUSE OF THE **RASCALS** WHOM ARE STEAL FROM ME SO I WARN THEM **STAY AWAY** OR I **SHOOT** I SAY.....NON?

7-16

WILEY CATT IS STEAL MY **RUTABAGAS!** I WARN HIM! I LOAD THESE GUN WITH THOSE **ROCK SALTS!** I HEAR NOISE IN NIGHT! I PULL **TRIGGER!**

BUT, UNFORTUNATE, THESE NOISE IS ONLY **YOU**....

GEE.... I'M SORRY.

YA MEAN YOU'D KILL A MAN FOR STEALIN' **RUTABAGAS,** MISS?

THE GUN WAS ONLY LOADED WITH **ROCK SALT.**

IT'S **SAFER** TO GET KILLED BY ROCK SALT?

MUCH SAFER.... **COME!** WE HAVE SOME SUPPER.

CHAPTER 21

THE WEIGH OF HER HEART

106

A REAPPRAISAL OF AGONY

As Secretary of Peace I've come to the conclusion that the conclusion of War will be the conclusion of all.

HUH?

FORT MUDGE MEMORIAL DUMP

I AGREE WITH POGO.

7-29

According to this old Almanac for 1816 we fought our best battle two weeks **after** the War of 1812 was over~~~

Those people had **perseverance**~~~ They understood War was their business~~~ yet they accepted **Peace**~~~ haugh!

HOW COME YOU SAYS HAUGH?

What did they accomplish with **Peace?**~~~ Today they're all **dead**~~~

ALL?

What job does Mole give *me* in this new cabinet? Secretary of Peace~~~ Haugh!

7-30

The new country doesn't want Peace~~~ People enjoy **WAR**~~~ It's very enlivening!~~~ And whom did Mole appoint as President? **A nothing**~~~ so meaningless that I forget who he was~~~

Some dull middle of the road clod---- what's his name? ----A dupe really, a malleable mental minus----

HIM.

FORT MUDGE MEMORIAL DUMP

When I said the President of our new country was a complete jackass, I forgot it was you, Pogo---- Pardon!

I'M MORE *INCOMPLETE*, HUH, DEAC?

LOOK!

7-31

WHY DON'T YOU AN' POGO JUST *SWAP JOBS?* YOU BE **PRESIDENT** AN' **POGO** BE SECRETARY OF PEACE?

Such a decision requires agonizing reappraisal---- Long hours of self examination----A man needs lengthy and noble and soulful inner commune.

I accept----

NOW IT'S COMPLETE

My first act as President will be to inform my minions that I am President---

A P.R. JOB, PREXY... LEAVE IT TO ME.

8-1

I'll say something simple like --- The finger of fate pokes forth and touches the outstanding man and appoints---

SAY SOMETHING THAT MEANS SOMETHING TO THE **PEOPLE**--- "WE HOLD THESE TRUTHS TO BE SELF-EVIDENT, THAT ALL MEN ARE CREATED EQUAL, THAT..."

A pretty sentiment---but I'd have to have the research team compute that out and verify it--- Now where was I?

FORT MUDGE MEMORIAL DUMP

Z

WHAT YOU NEED, DEACON, IS A **QUIT CLAIM DEED** THAT SHOWS YOU NOW OWNS THE JOB OF **PRESIDENT**.

Right.

8-4

" THIS CERTIFIES WHEREAS AND TO WIT THAT WHEREFORE I, THE PRESIDENT, HEREBY RESIGN TO BECOME SECRETARY OF PEACE, THEREFORE AFORESAID HITHERTO SEC'Y---

WOOF!

(WAIT, THERE'S **MORE**...) "...IS NOW AND HENCEFORTH PRESIDENT OF ALL I SURVEY, IPSO FACTO, INTO, OF AND WITH THE FUTURE AND BEYOND SO BE IT..."

COMPLETELY INCOMPREHENSIBLE!

Right, Pogo! **Magnificent!** Absolutely exquisite, legal phrasing---

I USED THE LAW LIBERRY A LOT DURIN' MY TENURE AT OSSINING.

I go forth to face Mole and all those rascals---As *President!*

BOY!

8-5

IF YOU THINK **I'M** GONNA SIGN THAT DOPEY DOCUMENT TRANSFERRIN' THE PRESIDENCY TO DEACON, YOU'RE WELCOME TO **ANOTHER THINK.**

RIGHT. EASY... POGO.

I DON'T WANT TO BE ASSOCIATED WITH **ANY** SUCH DESECRATION OF THE ENGLISH LANGUAGE!

I AGREE! YOU'RE A **BUSY MAN**--- *I SIGNED IT*...

♪

...FOR YOU.

111

CHAPTER 23

AN IRREVERSIBLE REVERSE

CHAPTER 24

THE PRESERVING PERVERSITY
OF PERSEVERANCE

HOW ABOUT **YOU** TWO? WANNA HELP STAMP OUT A LITTLE **HOLOCAUST**?

WELL, WHAT'S THE **PRESENT PLAN**? WHAT'RE **YOU** DOIN'?

AS YOU SEE, **I'M** CARRYIN' THE **HOSE**.... **YOU** ARE THE **FIRE CHIEF**!

I'M ALSO **SEC'Y** OF **PROBLEMS** AN' I AN' MY ASSISTANT IS IN EXECUTIVE SESSION....

Y' GOTTA REFER THE **FIRE** TO COMMITTEE.

WE'LL DO YOU A FAVOR... WE'LL **TABLE** THE CONFLAGRATION MOMENTARILY.... BUT PUT IT IN THE **URGENT BASKET**.... WE'LL TAKE IT UP NEXT SESSION....

FAIR ENOUGH.

IN 1971?

WHERE WAS WE? OH, YEAH! TRYIN' TO FIND A RHYME FOR **NATION**...

WHAT'S WRONG WITH THE FIRE SERGEANT'S SUGGESTION? HE HOLLERED OUT "**CONFLAGRATION**!"

AN' VERY GOOD, TOO.

8-13

WASTIN' TIME! A CHAMPION **FIRE** BURNIN' DOWN THE METROPOLITAN AREA AN' YOU GUYS IS STILL WRITIN' A **ANTHEM!**

YOU'RE JES' LIKE ALL THEM OTHER **REBEL YOUTH** DISTURBIN' DUE PROCESS OF GOV'T... WHAT BIG FAT DOPEY BUILDING **IS BURNIN'?**

OUR FIREHOUSE.

WHAT'S IN THE **FIREHOUSE** THAT'S WORTH **ANYTHING?** A ENGINE WHAT DON'T WORK... A AXE WITH NO HEAD... WATER WHAT'S NOT WET AN'...

BUT!

8-14

YOU **FORGET** OUR SPECIAL FIRE FIGHTIN' EQUIPMINTS --- OUR NECESSITIES... STUFF THAT YOU, **THE CHIEF,** ADORES IN FABLED STORY AN' SONG!

OUR **CHECKERS,** OUR **PINOCHLE** CARDS, OUR DARTS, OUR **FLOATIN' TOYS** FOR THE BATH, OUR OLD **CHEW'N GUM.**

HEY... HOW 'BOUT OUR WORK ON THE **ANTHEM?**

A PUBLIC OFFICE IS A **PUBLIC TRUST.**

118

WAIT A MINUTE ··· HERE'S **FIREHOSE**: .06 per foot. (complete extinguishment, .07½ per foot)··· NICE BARGAIN RATE THERE···

HAW! WHAT **FOR** DO YOU CARRY THE HOSE?

SERGEANT, IS YOUR HOSE **ON FIRE**? ··· MMM ··· **GUESS NOT** ··· THIS **IS** A PROBLEM.

THAT'S WHAT FOR I CARRY THE HOSE···

BE OF GOOD CHEER, MEN, WE'LL GET THIS FIRE **OUT YET** ··· NOW THE RATE ON A **TOOL** SHED FIRE IS QUITE NICE ···

HEY, **CHIEF!**

8-23

HERE'S A NICE FIRE EXTINGUISHMENT RATE ON A **POMERANIAN PUP TENT** ··· THE METHOD ALSO LEAVES A NICE BLAZE BURNIN' ON THE REAR STOOP IN CASE ONE WISHES TO PREPARE **BREAKFAST** ···

CHIEF!

WHAT!?

THE **RAIN** PUT THE FIRE OUT.

Y'SEE, BUN RAB ··· PERSEVERANCE! **PER-SEE-VERANCE** ··· IT'LL PAY YOU TO CURB YOUR HASTY NATURE.

© 1969 WALT KELLY

119

CHAPTER 25

A REIGN OF RAIN

8-21.

CHAPTER 26

BY DAWN'S EARLY
AND LATEST LIGHT

125

HOW COME YOU IS FISHIN' AROUND FOR A NEW ANTHEM?

ALBERT COULDN'T HIT THE **TOP** NOTES.

JUS' AS WELL, YES?

SO THEY WAS GONNA START A **NEW COUNTRY**.

L8-28

BUT THESE ARE WHAT IS GOOD ABOUT HER, **THESE ANTHEM...ALL** MUS' SING **TOGETHERS,** GIRLS, BOY, LADIES, MANS!

SOMEBODIES REACH ALL **EVERY** NOTES! MARCHONS, MES ENFANTS...*UN! DEUX!*

♪ *OH, SAY CAN YOU...* ♪

THE STAR SPANGLE BANNER ... **NOT** THE MARSEILLAISE, MISS MA'M'SELLE.

OOH... OUI! I KEEP FORGET.

TO OUR HOST, POGO, WHO AIN'T HERE BECAUSE HE'S ABSENT BUT LONG MAY HE WAVE.

8-29

♪ AND WHERE IS THAT BAND WHO SO VAUNTINGLY SWORE... ♪

126

THE INCOMPLEAT POGO

The poets have muddied all the little fountains.
Yet do not my strong eyes know you, far house? ...
                              Antara, 6th century.

For my father

The
INCOMPLEAT
POGO

CHAPTER 1

FROM HERE ON DOWN
IT'S UPHILL ALL THE WAY

Panel 1:
LOOKY AT **THAT!** WE RASSLED ALL AWAY DOWNHILL.... AN' IT STOPPED RAININ'....

AN' **YOU** IS LOST YO' EYE GOGGLES.

Panel 2:
C'MON.... I GOTTA GIT ON HOME AN' PUT ON A **FRESH** PAIR... CAN'T SEE SO GOOD....

Panel 3:
HEY, THAT'S **POGO'S** HOUSE; **NOT YOURN**.

HOW **CRUDE!** **DEE**-RIDIN' A MAN WHAT CAN'T SEE.

POGO

Panel 4:
BESIDES... **WHO** CAN TELL WHEN IT'LL START POURIN' **TORRENTS** AGAIN? YOU WANNA GIT **SOAKED?**

OH, WELL— I IS THE HOSPITABLE TYPE; I'LL **JOIN** YOU.

COOKIES

Panel 5:
SOON AS WE RESTS A BIT HERE AT **POGO'S**, US'LL GIT ON WITH OUR TRIP OVER TO MY HOUSE AN' GIT MY **GLASSES.**

POGO GOT A HOUSE LIKE A **SAM BERNARD** DOG.... IT ALLUS GOT A LI'L SOMETHIN' WITH IT.

Panel 6:
WITHOUT MY GLASSES, YOU LOOKS **DIFFERNT** ...FUZZY AN' **LUMP-**SIDED

FUNNY, TO ME, **YOU** LOOKS JUS' AS UGH AS EVER....

I ACCEPTS YO' **REE**-MARK AS THE **CRUDITY** OF A **IGNORHINOCERUS!** —— **MY SAKES!** POGO SURE PACKED IN SOME **AWFUL** TASTELESS GRUB.

YOU IS EATIN' YO' OWN HAT.

I IS HAD ABOUT ENOUGH! **YOU** IS SAYIN' I GOT A **BAD TASTE** IN HATS! **YOU IS A WALL-EYED OYSTER!**

A INSULT! I CHALLENGE YOU TO A LIFETIME OF BITTER HATRED.

AS THE FIRST STEP IN OUR **LIFETIME FEUD,** I CHALLENGE YOU TO A **CHECKER GAME** WITH COOKIES.

WINNER TAKE **ALL!**

IN AS MUCH AS WE IS PLAYIN' IN **POGO'S** HOUSE WITH **HIS** COOKIES AN' WITHOUT MY GLASSES, **HOUSE RULES** DICTATE THAT YOU GOTTA BE **BLINDFOLDED.**

I CAN BEAT YOU CRAWLIN', BLINDFOLDED, OR SICK ABED.

CAN'T SEE TOO GOOD.... IS YOU PROPER BLINDFOLDED?

NATCHERAL, I IS....WITH POGO'S NEW EASTER MORN NECKTIE....

AIN'T THAT A BIG, SHINEY, **DIS**-HONEST EYEBALL I SEES POOKIN' OUT.....? OR IS YOU WEARIN' A SET OF **FRIED EGGS**?

LET'S BE **FAIR**.... YOU NEVER SAID WHAT PART GOTTA GIT ALL KIVVERED.

IF YOU GONNA PLAY *FAIR*, YOU IS GOTTA BE BLINDFOLDED OVER THE BYEBONES.... *NOT ON THE MUSH!*

'LONG AS YOU CAN'T SEE WITHOUT YO' GLASSES, O.K.

YOO HOO

YES?

IT'S *ME*, GOOD OL' SEMINOLE SAM. I GOT A NEW LINE OF GOLDEN OPPORTUNITIES FOR OLD AN' YOUNG.

YOUR FRIEND HERE IS IN A EXCELLENT STATE TO GIVE MY PRODUCTS A *NOBLE* TRIAL.... A *BLINDFOLD* TEST OF PERIODICALS.

WE'LL TRY HIM OUT ON *COMIC BOOKS* FIRST.... *RIFFLE THRU THAT*, SIR .....IT IS ALIVE WITH CHUCKLE, PERIL, AND FLAMING LOVE........SAVOR ITS CRUNCHY GOODNESS, FRIEND.....WEIGH ITS *LIVELY MEATINESS....*

IT SOUND JES' FINE.

WULL.... IF I *GOTTA* CHOOSE, I THINK MEBBE *THIS* ONE'S FUNNIEST.

HA! NOW I'LL WARRANT YOU IT'S THE BRAND WHICH *I* ADVOCATE.... ...YES, CLASS *WILL TELL....*

OOP! SORRY! MISTAKENLY, I HANDED YOU *MY* COPY OF THE *CONGRESSIONAL RECORD.* OUR FACTORY IS CONSIDERING ILLUSTRATING IT IN COLOR... -PANEL BY PANEL--- *EXCELLENT CHOICE, BUT NOT READY...* COME, LET'S TRY AGAIN, SIR.

Panel 1 (Pogo): HEY, OL' CHURCHY! HEY, SEMINOLE SAM! HEY, HOWLAND OWL! HEY!

Panel 1 (Sam): HEY, YO'SELF, POGO.... I IS GIVIN' *CHURCHY* A BLINDFOLD TEST TO SELL HIM A *COMICAL BOOK.*

Panel 1 (Owl): A *BLINDFOLD TEST*? WHY, HE CAN'T *SEE* THE COMIC BOOK THAT WAY!

Panel 1 (Sam): AN' YOU BE SURPRISED WHAT A *BIG* HELP THAT *IS!*

Panel 2 (Sam): FOR A CHANGE, SAM, YOU IS RIGHT.

Panel 2 (Sam): YOU'LL HELP A *FINE, HANDSOME* BOY THRU *COLLEGE* IF YOU SUBSCRIBE, SIR.

Panel 2 (Churchy): LONG TIME NO SEE

Panel 2 (Pogo): ?

Panel 3 (Pogo): *WHAT* BOY?

Panel 3 (Sam): ME... AN' I'LL THROW IN A FREE BLINDFOLD...EACH TIME THIS COMES IN YOU PUTS ON YOUR BLINDFOLD...THEN YOU DON'T GOTTA PAY IT NO MORE MIND. THAN THE *AUTHOR* DID..

Panel 3 (Churchy): I SAID: LONG TIME NO SEE.

Panel 3: AN' I REPEATS:

Panel 3: ?

Panel 4 (Pogo): SO YOU'RE WORKIN' YOUR WAY THROUGH COLLEGE SELLIN' COMIC BOOKS?

Panel 4 (Sam): YES, INDEED...THE *ELECTORAL COLLEGE*... A OLD IVORY COVERED INSTITUTE.

Panel 5 (Pogo): I DON'T WANT TO BE STUPID BUT HOW CAN YOU SELL *COMICS* BY BLINDFOLDIN' THE CUSTOMER?

Panel 5 (Sam): THE *BLINDFOLD* TEST IS UNBIASED AN' TRUE... *TRY IT!*

CHAPTER 2

OUR HERO DOTS ONE EYE
AND CROSSES THE OTHER,
HAND OVER HAND

THIS COMIC BOOK I BOUGHT OFF'N OL' FOX SHOWS HOW WE GOES UP TO MARS, BRINGS BACK SOME MARTIANS AN' THEY *DEE*-STROYS THE *WHOLE EARTH!*

WHAT *NONSENSE!* BRINGIN' MARTIANS BACK.

WE'LL NEVER NEED *THEIR* HELP.

BOY! THAT'S A RELIEF.

SOMETHING THAT I HAVE FOR SALE MAY *INTEREST* A *BUSY MAN* LIKE *YOU*, SIR... HAVE YOU EVER GIVEN A THOUGHT TO *TOMORROW?*

ONLY WHEN IT FALLS ON A *SUNDAY.*

NOW, I GOT A LITTLE *SICK*NESS INSURANCE POLICY HERE.... S'POSE *TOMORROW*, AT THE *CRANK* OF *DAWN*, YOU GOTTA GIT UP AN' GO TO *WORK...*

OOG..!

YOU GOT A WIFE AN' *NINETEEN CHILLUN* *PLUS* A *GRAM'PA* AN A *SPECKLE DOG* TO SUPPORT... *BUT WHEN THE ALARM GO OFF THERE YOU IS... SICK!*

OOG... YOU AIN'T FOOLIN'.

YOU IS *MORTAL ILL!* GOTTA STAY IN BED FOR THE REST OF YO' *NATIONAL-BORN* LIFE.... NEVER DO A STROKE OF WORK AGIN.

GEE, THAT'S BETTER....... FOR A MINUTE YOU HAD ME *WORRIED..*

IF YOU IS *SICK* AN' CAN'T SUPPORT YO' *GRAMPA*, YO' *MISSUS*, NINETEEN *CHILLUN*, AN' THE *DOG*.... *THIS POLICY SWINGS INTO ACTION*..

'A DOCTOR COMES IN AN' *PATCHES* YOU UP...'*FORE* YOU KNOWS IT, YOU IS *UP* AN' ON YO' WAY *BACK* TO WORK!'

I *KNOWED* THERE WAS A *CATCH* IN IT!

YOU GOTTA THINK OF THE *FUTURE*, SIR...DON'T YOU EVER PLAN FOR A *RAINY DAY*?

NO, I USUAL LETS 'EM COME 'LONG BY THEY SELFS.

YOU IS *IMPROVIDENT*. HOW CAN YOU TELL WHAT THE DAY AFTER TO-MORROW MAY BE?

IF IT'S ANY-THING EXCEPT *JAN. 28*, I IS GONNA WRITE A *NASTY* LETTER TO THE CALENDAR COMPANY.

MY DEAR SIR, *WHY* DO YOU NOT WISH TO PLAN FOR A *RAINY DAY*?

AW, THEY AIN'T NO USE IN *THAT*, SAM...I PLANS ON NOTHIN' BUT THE *BEST*.....*SUNSHINE* AN' FOUR SQUARE MEALS A DAY....

THE S.S. COLIN HAWORTH

THE *GUMMINT* NEEDS A MAN LIKE YOU IN THE *RAINY DAY DEP'T*.

I IS *GUMMER-MENTAL TIMBER*, I ALLUS' SAY.

143

144

CHAPTER 3

WEATHER FORECAST:
TIARA BOOM-DE-AY
IN THE AFTERNOON

CHAPTER 4

MOLE BLOOMS
IN A SPRAY OF MYOPIA

YOU MEAN "EXAGGERATION." AWK!

I KNOW WHAT I MEAN.

I'M NOT *SO* NEAR SIGHTED BUT WHAT I'D OF *NOTICED* IT IN THE MIRROR IF I HAD DIED.

HOW?

YOU'RE JUST IN TIME, MOLE.... OL' SAM IS SELLIN' ALBERT THE *CINCINNATI* POST BUILDIN'... ALBERT'S GONE USE IT FOR A *WEATHER FACTORY*.... TO MAKE GOOD *U.S.* AN' *A.* TYPE OF WEATHER.

EXCELLENT IDEA... WE NEED *BETTER* WEATHER THAN CANADA'S BEEN SENDING US ..... *THEIR* EXPORT WEATHER IS SHODDY! *SHODDY!*

SLEEZY STUFF IN WINTER... NO *BODY* TO IT.....WEARS THIN IN *NO* TIME ---. AND THEIR SUMMER STOCK IS LAUGHABLE (*HA HA*). AN INTERNATIONAL *FRAUD!* TAKE THE GULF STREAM ... .*HAH!*

AIN'T THE GULFSTREAM OUR OWN JOB?

I'D ADVISE YOU TO WASH YOUR MOUTH OUT WITH SOAP, *DEAR BOY*..... *THAT* STREAM IS FROM THE GULF OF *MEXICO! HAH!* ABSOLUTELY UNREGULATED--! WANDERING *WILLY NILLY* ALL OVER OUR SOVEREIGN OCEAN .... A *SCANDAL!*

JUST ONE QUESTION, MY SON. **WHY** IS ALBERT GOING TO MANUFACTURE WEATHER IN A **FOREIGN** CITY......? CINCINNATI **INDEED**! WHY GO TO GREECE?

CINCINNATI AIN'T OVER IN GREECE.

DON'T USE **AIN'T**... WHEN I SAY: **IS** ... AN' STOP PICKING ON AN' OL' MAN WHAT CAN HARDLY SEE! A CIVIL TONGUE, YOUTH, A **CIVIL** TONGUE!

COULD IT **BE** THAT YOU'RE **AFRAID** TO ANSWER? PASS THE FISH, LAD.... BRISKLY DOES IT.

HE PICKED CINCINNATI 'CAUSE IT'S THE PLACE WHAT GOT A VERY FINE MEAN TEMPERATURE.

MEAN, EH? THAT'S THE **FLIMSY** TYPE WE BEEN GETTING FROM **CANADA** ... A CARTEL, NO DOUBT, OF INTERNATIONAL ALLIGATORS ... PASS THE BOTTLE OF CHUTNEY, BOY...

US DON'T 'LOW NO DRINKIN' TYPE LICKER IN HERE, MOLE.

NO **CHUTNEY**? ACK! IN THAT CASE, I'LL NEED ANOTHER FISH.. ...A CRISPY GOLDEN BROWN ONE ...

YOU ET 'EM ALL.

A SHAME! YOU DIDN'T EVEN SAVE **ONE** FOR YOUR GOOD COMPANIONS... MR. FOX OR MR. ALLIGATOR? **VERY** THOUGHTLESS, YOUNG MAN.

HEY.

BUT YOU WAS HUNGRY.

HEY, POGO! LOOK WHAT I GOT... UH... HELLO, MOLE. HEY, POGO LOOK WHAT I ...

AH! A BOTTLE OF CHUTNEY, AT LAST.

WHAH!? AN AMBUSH! A PIECE OF PETTIFOGGERY! A LOW AN' A CRAVEN GULLERY! IS THIS A KNAVISH COVIN?

NOSSIR, THAT'S OL' CLIFFORD, MY PET CRAWFISH...

A GEORGIA BOY.

IF I COULD BUT SIGHT THIS BRUMMAGEM BRANCHIOPOD I'D THUMP HIM A GOOD ONE.

IT'S YOUR CRAWFISH-- SHOULDN'T YOU CALL HIM?

MULL..

HAUGH! YOU VULTURE! FIGHT FAIR!

I'D CALL HIM BUT IT MERE MAKES HIM MAD IF I DO...

WHY?

'CAUSE I CALLS HIM: HO, CLIFFORD! HEY, THERE CLIFFORD! HERE, BOY! COME ON, CLIFFORD-- WHUP! WHUP!

WHAT'S WRONG WITH THAT?

CLIFFORD AIN'T RIGHTLY HIS NAME.

BEWARE! I AM ABOUT TO CHARGE, YOU POLTROON.

156

ALL RIGHT, SAM. *THERE'S* THE SHILLIN'....... THE *MEXICAN SHILLIN'*...

AN' NOW YOU ARE *SOLE* POSSESSOR OF MY INTEREST IN THE CINCINNATI POST BUILDING.

I'LL GIVE THE COIN A *TEST*...... *AOUGH!* IT TASTES *TERRIBLE*...

HAW! NOTHIN' BUT A *COUGH-DROP!* MINTAGE OF 1927.. ....*I FOXED YOU OUTEN YO' INTEREST!*

HA! WAIT'LL YOU PUT THE BITE ON THE *POST!*

I NEVER HAD NO INTEREST IN THAT BUILDING *ANY-WAYS*.... PREFERRED A THEATRE DOWN THE STREET-- SO *THERE!*

YOU OWES ME A UNGUMMED COUGHDROP.

LOST MY EYEGLASSES IN A BITTER BATTLE WITH A *CRUSTACEAN!* A *CRAWFISH* YCLEPT *CLIFFORD.*

LOOKIN' FOR 'EM, HUH?

YAWP!

I FOUND 'EM! BENT IN THE FRACAS, NO DOUBT.... BUT STILL CLEAR AS A CRYSTAL .... *20·20*

UH... YOU IS MORE FOUND **CLIFFORD**, MR. MOLE...

DON'T SEE HOW YOU CAN SEE THRU HIM, *DIRTY AS HE IS.*

HE *IS* A TRIFLE TIGHT, TOO...

WHO DOES *EITHER* OF YOU KNOW IN **CINCINNATI**? FELLA IS SENT YOU A PACKAGE AN' A HANDWROT LETTER.

IT'S FROM A *EDITOR* GO BY NAME OL' DICK THORNBURG... IT SAY: *DEAR HONORABLE SIRS: PLEASE ACCEPT THESE TOKENS OF OUR ESTEEM. YRS TRULY ETC.*

A **KEY**... LABELED *KEY TO THE CITY*---- MMM-- KEY TO THE CITY OF **FORT MUDGE**?

RIGHT NEXT DOOR.

YRS TRULY *ETC.*? WHO'S I KNOW NAME OF *ETC.*?

AN' A FRAMED MOTTO: "*THERE AINT NO EVER-LOVIN' BLUE EYED PLACE LIKE HOME.*"

YOU THINK HE'S IM-PLYIN' ANY-THING?

HE MUSTN'T OF KNOW HOW TO SPELL HIS **NAME!** PHOO ON *ETC.*

CHAPTER 5

WHEREIN OUR HERO LEARNS
THAT HOSPITALITY
IS MERELY MORTAL

WE NEED ★ *TALENT* ★ FOR THE 🖝 BIG TOP! IN FACT, HEADLOCK, WE NEED A BIG TOP!!!

WHERE'S THE LI'L BABY CHICK YOU ADOPTED?

Ah, I GROOMED HIM WELL!!! 🖝 *The Rooster Aerialist!* A RARE ★★ BIRD 🖝

A REAL SHOW-MAN? HE'LL BE BACK, EH?

Well, no.... He got illusions.. I put him on *in EL PASO* ...HE LAID AN 🖝 egg! 🖝 *Blamed* it on Atmospheric CONDITIONS ---- BUT HE ! LOOKED ! PROUD 🖝 NONETHELESS !!

PROMISED NOT TO DO IT *A-GAIN!* BUT I NEVER KNEW WHEN..... AND HIM UP OVER THE CROWD ON A HIGH WIRE ∼∼∼ *WELL!* YES, MERMSIE, my boy, he went to pot ∼∼∼

HOW WAS HE?

Oh, if only some truly ★ *STELLAR* ! attraction ! *would come my way*

WE'LL TIPPE CANOE OVER TO *POGO'S* AN' EASE CLIFFORD INTO A CUP OF SASSY-FRASH TEA AN' IT'LL PUT HIM TO SLEEP AN'..

HOW'D YOU LIKE TO BE A GREAT CLOWN? *Outward all laughs?* BUT INWARD DYIN' OF A *BROKING HEART?* HOT DOG!

RIGHT! EVERYBODY WOULD LAUGH *BUT* → INSIDE ← *you is all* TRAGEDY ☆ (*a little* SOFT MUSIC, SOUSA)

HOW 'BOUT TAGGER RIG?

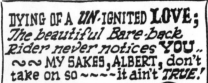

DYING OF A *UN*-IGNITED LOVE; *The beautiful Bare-back Rider never notices* YOU.. ~ ~ MY SAKES, ALBERT, *don't take on so* ~~~-*it ain't* TRUE!

YOWP! YOWP!

AW, I WASN'T TAKIN' ON~~... I WAS HOLLER'N' 'CAUSE OL' CUMQUOTH HERE WAS HITTIN' *ME* 'STEAD OF THE DRUM~~ UH...WHAT'S THIS JOB LIKELY TO PAY?

PIERROT OL' BOY, US THOUGHT YOU WAS BEIN' THIS CLOWN FOR *LAUGHS.*

ALBERT, my boy, A CAREER of FAME-STUDDED *Stardom* awaits → *YOU* ☆ ~~~ YOUR PLACE *is on the* TANBARK *with the pleasaunt cry of* "HEY RUBE" WAFTED ON THE SUMMER AIR!!!!

WELL, C'MON IN AN' SET A SPELL ---- I IS EXPECTIN' *POGO*... HE'LL HELP ME DECIDE. *MEANWHILES US'LL SNACK A BIT.*

IF'N I GOES OFF WITH THE **CIRCUS** WHAT'LL POOR POGO DO WITHOUT ME? I SORTA LOOKS AFTER HIM.

Why, **YOU** are . the ⟡ **SOUL** ⟡ of **GENEROSITY,** ☆ ☆ **ALLOW THE** *poor waif* to lodge here in **YOUR ABSENCE!!**

SURE.... ALL THIS STUFF YOU'RE GIVIN' **US** COULD BE HIS ....YOU SEEM TO GOT PLENTY.

IT'S *ALREADY HIS.* THIS HERE IS **POGO'S** PLACE ...

OOP, S'CUSE ME ... DIN'T MEAN TO BLUNDER INTO NO **RESTAURANT.**

C'MON IN, POGO, YOU IS WELCOME. HAPPEN THIS IS **YOUR** PLACE.

SON, US IS CELEBRATIN' A **BIG** OPPORTUNITY! **FAME** AND **FORTUNE!** THE **NAME** IN **LIGHTS** .... **TALENT IN FULL FLOWER!**

Gay **CIRCUS LIFE** *BECKONS!!* *The* **APPLAUSE** *of Thousands!* **LAUGHTER! Song!** Cheers *on every* ⟡ Hand ⟵ !! DOES THAT **SOUND** *Acceptable,* SIR?

GOSH, I DUNNO, I'M OVERCOME... I· UH·· WELL, YES.

FINE! *THAT'S ALL, POGO!* I ACCEPTS, P.T., GET OUT THE CONTRACK AN', POGO, PUT ON MORE COFFEE AN' SEE KIN YOU BAKE UP A CAKE.

CHAPTER 6

BRAINS FROM FAR AND WIDE
ARE SUMMONED TO PONDER
A SUICIDE PACK

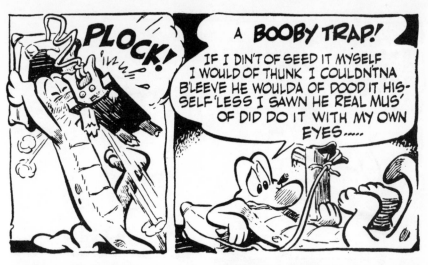

PLOCK!

A **BOOBY TRAP!** IF I DIN'T OF SEED IT MYSELF I WOULD OF THUNK I COULDN'TNA B'LEEVE HE WOULDA OF DOOD IT HIS-SELF 'LESS I SAWN HE REAL MUS' OF DID DO IT WITH MY OWN EYES.....

WITH THIS **GARBAGE** HANGIN' OUTEN MY BAG, FOLKS'LL THINK I DON'T KNOW HOW TO **PACK!** ----I'LL GO BACK IN AN' **CLIP OFF** THE **HANGOVERS.**

OW! DAG NAG THAT POGO....I FERGOT 'BOUT HIM HAVIN' THAT **MISSIN' DOORSTEP!**

OR ...UM, LET'S SEE... I FERGOT 'BOUT HIM **NOT** HAVIN' A MISSIN' DOOR-STEP...

STILL HOW COULD HE **NOT** HAVE IT IF HE **DO** BUT HOW COULD HE **DO** IF ...**YAWK!**

BY JING! HE DOGBONE WELL BETTER GIT IT FIXED! GOT IT OR **NOT!**

172

I ASK **CLIPPED** QUESTIONS, SIR---- IF THE DOG'S GONE HE'S MISSIN' OR DEAD? WHO? WHICH?

I DUNNO! EVER'BODY WAS **NUTS** ABOUT HIM.

THE CASE IS BLOCKED! "EVER'BODY WAS NUTS!" THAT PART OF THE REPORT MAKES ME THINK! AS A COP I'M THROWIN' EVERY BRAIN IN MY HEAD INTO THIS.

AS LONG AS WE'RE **SHORT HANDED** I'LL GO GET **HELP!**

HEY, HOUN'DOG, C'MON AN' **HELP!** SOMETHIN' MUST IS HAPPENED TO **PUP DOG.** I LEFT HIM TIED UP... COULD YOU SNIFF OUT THE TRAIL?

GLADLY AN' IN DUTI- BALLY.

ALBERT STOPS BY.. SEES I LEFT OL' PUP TIED TO THE DOOR STEP---- ALBERT PICKS UP A SUITCASE... **PFFFT!** THE PUP IS **GONE!**

HAS OL' ALBERT STILL GOT THE GRIP?

NO, JUS' A LI'L' COUGH... HE FEEL JUS' FINE.

NO MORE OF THAT! THAT IS, IF YOU WANTS MY KEEN NOSE ON THE JOB... STUFFED THO' IT IS WITH **PNEUMONIA.**

YOU DON'T SMELL AS GOOD AS YOU DID?

GROWL.

CHAPTER 7

THE CASE IS OPEN
AND/OR SHUT AT WILL

IT'S JUST A "FOR-INSTANCE-YOU." A "YOU" IN THE ABSTRACT.

BUT IT AIN'T GOT NO PERTY BROWN SPECKLE EYEBALLS.

CHECK! PERTY BROWN SPECKLE EYEBALLS--THE CASE IS OPEN FOR BUSINESS AGAIN, CHIEF.

NOW WE NEED A SUSPECT---MY NAME IS ALBERT. I'M OUT. THE PUP IS OUT... YOU'RE .... UM--- YOU'RE. ---- HM... YOU? WELL, YOU?

CLOSE THE CASE A MINUTE, CLOSE IT. WODDYA MEAN I'M A SUSPECT?

I DIN'T SAY FOR SURE... I ONLY SUSPECTS YOU IS A SUSPECT.

IF YOU'RE GONE SUSPECT ME, THE NOBLE DOG WITH-DRAWS FROM YO' ADMINISTRATION.

AW... COME ON! COME ON!

MY PROFESSIONAL DOG'S HEART IS SORE STUNG BY THE STINGS AN' NARROWS OF OUTRAGED FORTUNE.

I DIN'T MEAN NOTHIN' PERSONIAL. I WAS JES' NOT LEAVIN' NO WORMS UNTURNED.

THERE, THERE! LET'S OPEN THE CASE FOR BUSINESS AGAIN AS EQUAL PARTNERS! DO I HEAR YOU PURRIN' YOUR AGREEDIENTS?

DOGS DON'T HARDLY PURR AT ALL----- I'M THINKIN' THIS OVER.

COME ON IN, PORKY PINE. I IS GITTIN' READY TO GO OUT LOOKIN' FOR **PUP DOG!** HE'S CHECKED IN **MISSIN'** ---

UM, I WAS JES' ABOUT TO START MY **ANNUAL** SPRING-TIME COURTIN' OF MIZ HEPZIBAH AN' IS COME FER THE **BORRY** OF YO' MANDOLIN 'CAUSE MY BAGPIPES IS BUST.

HELP YO' SELF, SON. ALSO THERE IS A BOX OF CANDY I IS TOO **UN-BARRASSED** TO GIVE HER **LAST** YEAR.

HEY!'

(S'CUSE ME, MA'M--) 'FRAID THE CANDY IS STALE, POGO.

OH, WELL, SHE'LL GOTTA LOVE YOU FOR YO' MUSIC... Y'KNOW THIS GUN IS **HEAVY!**

UNLOAD HER--- I'LL CARRY THE POWDER AN' BALL AN' GIVE YOU A HAND LOOKIN' FOR THE PUP.

UNLOAD HER? IF SHE **WAS** LOADED I COULDN'T LIFT HER AT ALL--- BESIDES IT'S RISKY TO USE A LOADED GUN.

THERE'S OL' **P.T. BRIDGEPORT**--- ALBERT AGREED TO GO CIRCUSSIN' WITH HIM --- ONLY NOW ALBERT IS GOT SIDETRACKED PLAYIN' **COP** IN THE CASE OF THE **MISSIN' PUP DOG.**

Ah, Gentlemen, have you SEEN **ALBERT?** HE'S OVER-DUE AT THE **CIRCUS LOT** ∽ We must hit the **ROAD!**

SHERIFF TROUBLE?

YOU KNOW THE *FIRST THING* WE OUGHT TO FIND OUT 'BOUT THE *MISSIN'* PUP DOG?

SURE, WHERE IS HE.

WHAT KIND OF SLOPPY PO-LICE WORK IS *THAT*? YOU'RE GOIN' AT IT *ALL BACKWARDS!*

BACK-WARDS? AIN'T WE S'POSED TO FIND OUT WHERE IS HE?

FINDIN' *THAT* OUT COMES *LAST!* WHEN WE DO THAT THE CASE IS *DONE.* *NOW*, WHAT COMES AHEAD OF THAT?

ACTUAL, *WHO* STOLT HIM?

NOT SO FAST! FIRST, (TIME 11:17) WE FIGGER OUT *WHO* WE SUSPECKS. YOU GOTTA PROCEED SCIENTIFIC!

THIS HERE MYSTERY WAS A LOT SIMPLER WHEN IT ONLY HAD *ME* THINKIN' ABOUT IT.

CHAPTER 8

BRAINS, SIZE 6¼,
ARE POOLED TO FORM A
SHALLOW BUT SLIPPERY PUDDLE

ADD THAT UP, PARDNER. *TIME 1:12...Remarks: Both the Mole and the Pup Wasn't seen.*

IN OTHER WORDS: TOGETHER, THEY IS **MISSIN'!**

CHECK! AN' YOU CAN ADD, *(TIME 1:13½) The Mole ain't tak talkin'*

THE WAY **EVIDENCE** IS PILIN' UP, *IT IS POSITIVELY UNCANNY!*

IT'S SURE TOO DEEP FOR ME.... I NEED MY BOOTS.

I THINK ALBERT AN' BEAU-REGARD ARE ON THE **RIGHT TRAIL** .....IT LOOKS LIKE OL' MOLE DID IT ALLRIGHT.

DID WHAT?

SNATCHED THE **PUP DOG** OF COURSE...... HE'S PROB'LY A UNDERCOVER DOG CATCHER.

YOU AN' ALBERT AN' THE HOUN'DOG SURE BEEN **TALKIN'!**

YES, INDEED! WE'VE **DIS-**CUSSED, *RE-*CUSSED.... ALL WAS GIVE A FAIR CHANCE TO TALK AN' DEE-FEND MOLE ... BUT WE ENDED UP SUSPECTIN' HIM FAIR AN' SQUARE....

DID YOU HAVE TIME TO THINK?

ALL IN GOOD TIME .....WE AIN'T THE SLOPPY KIND WHAT TRIES TO DO **TWO** THINGS AT ONCE. *UP TO NOW WE BEEN JES' TALKIN'*...BUT WHEN WE START *THINKIN' 'BOUT THIS.. STAND BACK!*

JES' SO YOU DON'T FERGIT IT.

184

SOMEBODY'S LOOKIN' AT OUR PIT FALL ·· I'LL RUSH AROUN' ONE WAY···

AN' I'LL RUSH 'ROUN' T'OTHER···

··· AN' WE'LL COTCH HIM ATWIXT OF ····

····US.

WE GOT THIS MOLE FOOLED···HE THINKS WE GRABBED EACH OTHER ON PURPOSE, HA!

YEAH····SHHH·· LET'S SPRING ON HIM···PULL HIS COAT OVER HIS HEAD IN A DAZZLIN' DISPLAY OF JIMINY JITSU!

INTO THE BUSH!

GOT HIM! BUNDLE HIS HEAD IN HIS COAT!

YESSIR! *GOT HIM!* DAGNAB, LOOKY, HOUN'DOG! AIN'T OL' MOLE'S UNDER-PINNIN' A **RIDICULOUS** SIGHT?!

EVER'THIN' ALL RIGHT?

UH----OH, HULLO UNCLE BALDWIN! I GOT OL' MOLE HERE ---CAUGHT HIM RED HANDED----WHERE'S HOUN'DOG?

NO *MATTER!* HE **RUN OUT!** WE'LL FORCE A CONFESSION OUTEN MOLE.

GRAB THAT STICK! EVER'BODY TAKE TURNS **WHACKIN'** 'TIL MOLE TELLS US **WHERE PUP DOG IS!**

BUT, **ALBERT,** YOU DON'T **KNOW** IF MOLE TOOK PUP DOG.

DON'T GIMME THAT! MOLE **LOOKS** *GUILTY ENOUGH TO HANG*---GO AHEAD!

GUILTY OF **WHAT,** PRAY TELL?

YEAH, **O·KAY,** MOLE.... YOU'LL GIT YOUR TURN TO WHACK MOLE AN' MAKE MOLE TELL WHERE HE HID PUPDOG. SO JES' GIT IN LINE, MOLE, AN'...

MOLE!?

UM.

DOG BONE! YOU IS MOLE! THEN WHO'S I GOT **HERE?**

WHO, INDEED?

AN' **WHY,** TOO.?

BLESS MY SOFT BROWN EYES .... **IT'S BEAU-REE-GARD!**

TO **THINK** THAT **YOU,** MY FELLOW-SLEUTH, IS THE KIDNAPPER --

WHAT?

ALBERT! YOU SUSPECTS ONE MAN, CATCHES THE **WRONG** ONE AN' SO YOU CLAIMS THE ONE YOU **IS GOT** IS **GUILTY!** JUS' **CATCHIN'** A MAN DON'T PROVE HE'S A **CULPRIT!**

IT'S A GOOD **START..** AIN'T IT?

A VERY GOOD START.

188

189

190

A MEDIUM RARE DAY IN JUNE
IS WELL DONE

IT'S A JUMPY WAY OF LIFE, ANYWAYS.

I BEEN FIGGERIN' OUT WHAT YOU SAID----THAT WE AIN'T GOT NO *FIFTY FIRST* OF *OCTOBER.*

WHAT'S TO FIGGER OUT 'BOUT *THAT?*

ALL THE *FIFTY FIRSTS* OF *OCTOBERS* FALL ON THE *TWENTEETHS* OF NOVEMBERS.

OCTOBER STOP ON THE THIRTY ONE OF IT.

WHY?

YOU CAN'T GO HAVIN' A WHOLE *YEARFUL* OF OCTOBER.

WHY NOT..? IT'S A *PERTY* MONTH..... WE COULD HAVE OCTOBER, CHRISTMAS, THE FOURTH OF JULY AN' MY BIRTHDAY AN' LET ALL THE OTHER MONTHS GO......... *FEBRUARY FOR INSTINCT... WHO* NEEDS IT?

192

JANUARY NEEDS IT··· KEEPS IT FROM BUNKIN' INTO MARCH!

COME COME -- LET US BE REALISTIC.

I THINK I GOT THE **NEW CALENDAR** **ALL** SET.

NEW CALENDAR?

YEP··· THE **OCTOBER CALENDAR**··· CHRISTMAS COMES ON THE **86**TH OF OCTOBER.

ONE GOOD MONTH ALL YEAR LONG. THE **FIRST** OF THE YEAR FALLS ON OCTOBER NINETY-THIRD···· WODDY YOU THINK OF THAT!

OH, I DUNNO·····IT'S ONE OF THEM THINGS I DON'T THINK ABOUT VERY MUCH.

CHAPTER 10

A FRIEND IS DRUNK
ON A SOBERING NOTE

IF YOU IS A *PERFESSIONAL* PREE-DICTER WHERE'D YOU PREEDICK AT AFORE?

I WORKED FOR A *NEW ORLEANS* NEWSPAPER.

H_2O

I WAS THE ORIGINAL *PICAYUNE FROG*... A WEATHER EXPERT... BUT THE BOSS, HONEST GEORGE, WAS A *HARD MAN*... MADE ME WEAR SHOES... SAID I WAS SOGGY AN' HE DIN'T LIKE HIS CARPETS ALL DAMPED... *THIS*, OF COURSE, MADE MY FEET HURT.....

H_2O

NATURAL, I PREDICKS *RAIN* FOR *SIXTY SEVEN DAYS*... OL' GEORGE SAT AT HIS DESK UNDER A UMBRELLA AN' CARRIED A LOADED LIGHTNIN' ROD AT ALL TIMES..... *WELL*, SIR! WE HAD SIXTY SEVEN DAYS OF *UN*-MITIGATED SUNSHINE....

HONEST GEORGE PEEKS OUT AN' HE *SEE*: SOMETHIN' IS WRONG. HE TOOK BACK THE COMP'NY SHOES, GUV *ME* THE SACK AN' BRUNG IN ANOTHER BOY... WHO *KNOWS, MEBBE A RELATIVE*... BUT ANYWAY A IMPOSTOR WHO COULDN'T PREDICK *Xmas* ON DEC. 24.

THAT IS OCTOBER 457th.

THIS *NEW ORLEANS* PAPER HELD A CONTEST TO SEE WHO'D BE THE *WEATHER MAN*... ME OR A *OUTLANDER* NAMED "*POGO*" (SAID TO HAVE SHARP WEATHER EARS.)

HA! ME AN' OL' GEORGE, THE HEAD MAN, FIXED *THAT!* WE BOLSTERED THE BALLOT BOX AN' I WAS A *SHOO IN!* ..... *ONLY LATER* DID I LEARN THAT THE JOB CARRIED *NO* SALARY.

196

I DENOUNCED THIS PENURIOUS ATTITUDE AND FOUND MYSELF AT *LIBERTY*...SO I PICKETED THE MARDI GRAS SINGLEHANDED... *GEORGE* CHARGED THAT I WAS NOT A *FROG* BUT A MIDGET *ALLIGATOR!* A VILE **SLANDER** !

ON **WHO**, HOPPY TOES ?

WHAT'S IN THE SATCHEL,YOU **SHORT** TAILED SALAMAGANDER?

I WOULDN'T TELL ANY OVERGROWED LIZARD...

NOTHIN' BUT WATER...

I COME OVER TO SET UP A FORECASTIN' BUREAU....

HAW.... I'LL JES' DRINK IT UP... I'LL LEARN HIM TO BE SO SMART.

I GOT A AMOEBA IN WATER... HE KNOWS *EVER'THIN'*

HE FORECASTS WEATHER AN' ...**HEY! YOU POT-EYED PLATTER-PUSS!** YOU DRUNK MY **FRIEND!**

CHAPTER 11

OWL GOES SLUMMING

I *KNOW* YOU IS A **BUSY MAN**, MR. PICAYUNE HOP FROG, BUT *HOW* COME YO' A-MOEBA HAS *H·2·O* ON HIS LI'L' SATCHEL?

IT'S HIS '*NITIALS*.

Y'SEE, I GOT ME A JOB BEIN' **ADVANCE MAN** FOR A **PELICAN** FROM UP **BATON ROUGE** WAY--- HE'S IN **SHOW BUSINESS** SO HE TELL ME: "GIT ON OUT WITH THE **ALL SEEIN'** AMOEBA WHAT KNOWS ALL AN' RUSTLE UP CROWDS..."

OL' AMOEBA GOT A NAME ON HIM WHAT SHOW HE KNOW *ALL* FROM **BE**GINNIN' TO *END*... YES **SIR!** **H**ALPHA 2 **O**MEEBA... KINDA OF A CARNIVAL A-RAB...... 2 IS FOR *TWO'S DAY*... HIS BIRTHDAY BEIN' THE SECOND DAY OF THE WEEK.

THOUGHT TUESDAY WAS THE *THIRD* DAY OF THE WEEK.

NO, YOU'RE THINKIN' OF *THIRD'S DAY*...COMES AFORE FRIDAY.....*DON'T* FEEL BAD, THO' 'TAIN'T NO DISGRACE TO BE STUPID.

WHAT'S THE STORY 'BOUT THIS PELICAN?

MUS' OF IS START *WAY* BACK. MAN, GO BY NAME OF **NAPOLEUM**, HE COME 'LONG AN' HE SAY TO TH' **PELICAN**, HE SAY, "*BOY*, HOW YOU LIKE TO BUY *LOU'SIANA*?"

HEE! HE MUS' OF TOLE NAPOLEUM "*GO BACK THAT FLITTER-FLY HOUSE!*" "HE COULDN'T OF BOUGHT LOUISIANA.

HE DID TOO BOUGHT IT! INCLUDIN' *NORTH* AN' SOUTH *DA-KOTA!*

CHAPTER 12

AN AFFAIR OF HONOR
IS AN INSIDE JOB

205

FIRST OF ALL, THO', I'LL GRAB UP A SWORD FROM MY AMMUNITION DUMP (FOR WORK IN **CLOSE QUARTERS**), BECAUSE, *VERY LIKELY*, TURTLE...

... WILL *HACK* HIS WAY **IN** AFTER ME AN' WE'LL HAVE A *WILD FREE-SWINGIN' SWORD FIGHT UP* AN' **DOWN** STAIRS!

SLUM THAT **SAM'WICH** DOWN IN **BACK** OF OWL 'CAUSE HIS **FRONT** IS *TICKLISH*.... HOPE YOU PUT PLENTY...UH-UH......

YEH.... I PUT *PLENTY*....

UH-UH

... PEPPER ON IT

CHAPTER 13

THE HOSE IS CARRIED
TO EXTREMES

210

I'D RUTHER BE BURNED UP THAN FISHED UP.

WITH MY METHODS YOU CAN HAVE BOTH--- NOW THEN, THE FISH---

HERE'S THE *LAST* OF THE *FISH* YOU FLUNG.

I CARRY THE HOSE.

WAIT 'TIL I *TALLY* 'EM UP.

WHAT'S YOU GOTTA *TALLY* UP? THEY WAS ONLY *THREE*.

NOW! NOW! YOU IS GIVE ME *TWO*... THIS ONE MAKES *THREE*.

HOLD HIM A MINUTE.... WHERE'S THE OTHER TWO--- AH, HERE ---WELL, *THAT ONE IS THREE*.. SO THIS ONE IS *FOUR*...THIS ONE IS *FIVE*...

SIX.

I CARRY THE HOSE.

SEE! *SIX!* IT PAYS TO TALLY UP, HOUN'DOG--- DON'T IT NOW?

CHAPTER 14

IN WHICH IT IS SEEN
THAT IT IS HARD TO HOLD
AS MUCH AS A PELICAN

PHOO -- ALL IS LOST.

LOST MY AMOEBA **WITH** THE **GOLD** TOOTH --- LOST MY SATCHEL AN'- - -

AN'--

AN' LOST YO' JOB, PICAYUNE! A *FINE ADVANCE MAN* YOU IS BEEN FOR ME!

ROOGEY BATOON! THE UNDENIABLE *PELICAN!* THE MAN WHO *MADE* THE LOU'SIANA PURCHASE...

HOW'D YOU DO IN THAT *CALAVERAS COUNTY JUMP,* CHAMP?

THEY THREW A *RINGER* AT ME.... A *NON-GUILD MEMBER*... HARDLY A FROG A- *TALL!*

I HAPPEN TO KNOW IT WAS A *SMALL SALT-LAKE CITY GRASS-HOPPER*... HE HOPPED YOU *BLIND!*

HE USED *WINGS!* HE *USED* WINGS!

SO DO *YOU*... IN THE *BAYOU*..! WATER WINGS!

YOU COULD USE YOUR *WINGS* A LI'L' AN' SAVE WEAR AN' TEAR ON **MY** *FEET BONES.*

POP INTO THE PAIL, POP IF YOU'RE POOPED.

THINK OF THE TROUBLE I IS SAVED YOU, POGO, BY HELPIN' YOU EAT THAT **DEE**-LICORICE **LUNCH** YOU PACKED...

UM!

YOO HOO!

VOICES FROM OUTEN THE *BLUES*....

IS US A-NOTHER MAID OF ORLEANS?

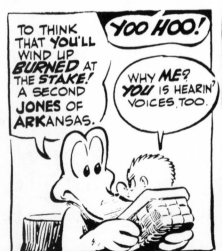

TO THINK THAT **YOU'LL** WIND UP **BURNED** AT THE **STAKE!** A SECOND **JONES** OF **AR**KANSAS.

YOO HOO!

WHY **ME?** **YOU** IS HEARIN' VOICES TOO.

I DON'T HEAR 'EM SO GOOD AS I DID.. TELL 'EM NOBODY ISN'T AT HOME.

YOO HOO!

DON'T LET'S US ANSWER ATALL... LET 'EM RING.... MEBBE THEY'LL CALL SOME BODY ELSE.

HEY DOWN THERE!

IF ONLY WE HAD SOMETHIN TO DROP TO SNARE THEIR ATTENTION.

GREAT IDEA, PICAYUNE.

THEM MYSTERIFUL VOICES FROM OUTEN NOWHERES.

BLOWNK

DID YOU HEAR A SORT OF A HOLLOW SOUND?

HEY! ALBERT!

SOMETHIN' IS STRUCK ME, POGO----- LET'S BEAT IT!

LET'S.

GOOD! WE IS EXCAPIN' SO FAST I IS ALMOST LOSIN' MY HAT!

HOT DOG!

CHAPTER 15

A BASS BARITOON, A CONTRALTOR
AND A TREBLE CLEFT PALATE

SEE HOW YOU LIKES THE **LOU'SIANA PERCHES** SINGIN' "A SLOOP IN THE DOOP."

SOUNDS KINDA *GURGLY*---SOMETHIN' IS THROWIN' 'EM OFF---I THINK ONE OF 'EM GOT A *FROG* IN HER THROAT.

SIR!

IF ONE OF THE SINGIN' **LOU'SIANA PERCHES** IS GOT A BAD THROAT IT'S FROM OVER-WORK---THEY NEEDS A REST.

THEY NEEDS A LITTLE **VACATION**---A CULTURAL TRIP TO **DR. BRENNAN'S UPSTAIRS WAXWORKS**--- OR A EDUCATIONAL TOUR OF THE **VIEUX CARRÉ**.

YOU FERGITS WE ISN'T IN N'ORLEANS.

RIGHT, PICAYUNE -- MEBBE YOU GENTS COULD SUGGEST A **GENTEEL** DIVERSION FOR THREE MAIDEN PERCHES?

THINK THEY'D LIKE TO GO **FISH!N**, POGO?

SHUSH, THEY *IS* FISH.

WULL---I GOT A CAN OF **BAIT** OVER'T MY PLACE. FIGGER THEY'D LIKE TO HELP *UNSNARL* A FEW YARDS OF **NIGHT CRAWLERS**?

IT'S QUIET BUT ABSORBIN' WORK.

MEBBE OL' **ROOGEY BATOON** IS RIGHT, HIS LI'L PERCH FISH SINGERS NEEDS A LITTLE FUN.

ALL WORK AN' NO PLAY MAKES **FLIM, FLAM AN' FLO** A DULL **QUAR**TET.

THEY'S ONLY THREE--- THEY'RE MORE A **TRIO**.

BUT FLAM GOT A **BANJO**--A OL' **HE**-BANJO WITH A VOICE LIKE A BURGLAR! **THAT'S** FOUR.

WHO DO WE KNOW COULD ESCORT THEM GAL FISH TO A **NIGHT BALL GAME** OR A SIMILAR **SOIRÉE?**

IT WOULD HAFTA BE THREE GENTS OF **MEANS** AN' **MANNERS** BUT ALSO A LI'L **BATS!**

THAT'S US--- **GANGWAY!**

WE'S PRACTICIN' UP FOR **HOLLOW-WEEN**- OUR **NATIONABLE** HOLIDAY.

HOW'D YOU BOYS LIKE TO HAVE A **DATE** WITH THREE BEAUTIFUL GIRL **SINGERS?**

IT'D BE KINDA **NOISY.**

YEAH, WITH THEM **HOOTIN'** AN' **HOLLOWIN'** UP A STORM.

AN' **SNAPPIN'** THEIR FINGER BONES.

FIGGER US WANT TO BOOK A TRIO OF **GROANERS?**

ASK HIM DO HE KNOW ANY **ACROBATS** OR **WOMBATS** OR SOMETHIN' FAMILIAR.

NOT **TOO** FAMILIAR.

WE'RE THINKIN' OF GETTIN' UP A *PURSE*, POGO, TO GIVE TO *ROOGEY BATOON* FOR HIS *PERCHES* WE ATE.

YEP, WE'RE GONNA SELL A *JOKE* TO ONE OF THEM *FUNNY* MAGAZINES.

THEN WE'LL GIVE THE MONEY TO *ROOGEY*... WE'LL DRAW A PICTURE OF A BIG *RADIO* AND *TEEVY WRITERS'* MEETING....

EVER'BODY IS LI'L' *CLOCKWORK MENS*.. ONE OF 'EM IS GITTIN' *WOUND* BY ANOTHER WHO IS GOT THE *KEY* IN THIS GUY'S *EAR*... AN' HE IS SAYIN'....

HOL' YO'SELF *IN NOW,* POGO.

WHOO OO-HEE.

YOOH-HA..*OOF-HAW*..HEE... AN' HE IS SAYIN': "*I KNEW WE WAS GITTIN'* MECHANICAL BUT I DIN'T KNOW WE WOULD *WIND UP LIKE THIS!*" AW..*HAWF..WIAH-HA..* WHEE...HOO *BOY!*

YEE HAW *YEOW!*

OO.. IT'S *SUREFIRE!*

CHAPTER 16

THE BITE OF THE REMEDY

POGO, DOES YOU REALIZE THAT **ROOGEY BATOON** IS BEEN *ET* RIGHT OUTEN BUSINESS?

HOWEVER, I IS GOT ANOTHER LINE.

I IS BRUNG ALONG A STOCK OF **SNAKE BITE MEDICINE** FOR SALE

ONLY TROUBLE WITH THAT IS US *NEVER* MEETS UP WITH *NO SNAKES.*

TRUE, SIR, TRUE TRUE. *AND SO....*

.... FOR THE ACCOMMODATION OF MY CUSTOMERS -- *BEE-HOLD.*

DOES YOU MAKE SNAKES BITE PEOPLE SO THEY'LL BUY YOUR **SNAKE BITE** REMEDY?

NOW, FRIEND..

THAT'S *HARDLY* THE WAY TO DESCRIBE MY SERVICE ... I GOT **SNAKE BITE CURE** FOR SALE.. *WHAT GOOD IS IT WITHOUT SNAKE BITE?*

230

FRIEND, *YOU* LOOK LIKE AN *HONEST* MAN... WOULD YOU RESPECT *ANY* MAN WHO SOLD YOU SOMETHIN' YOU DIDN'T *NEED?*

'COURSE NOT.

RIGHT! AND SO, FRIEND, I GO TO THE TROUBLE AN' *EXPENSE* OF GIVIN' YOU A *FREE* SNAKE BITE *BEFORE I SELL YOU A SINGLE DROP OF REMEDY!*

WHAT'S WRONG WITH *THAT?*

I'LL THINK OF SOMETHIN'

AS A SPECIAL INTRODUCIAL OFFER, I'M GONNA SELL YOU *TWO* BOTTLES FOR THE PRICE OF *ONE.*

NO, YOU'RE NOT..... I DON'T NEED *NO* SNAKE-BITE CURE.

GO AHEAD AN' *SNAP* 'EM UP, POGO ---- IT'S A *BIG BARGAIN* .... A THING LIKE THIS DON'T COME ALONG *EVERY DAY....*

THANK GOODNESS! I REPEATS: *I DON'T GOT NO* SNAKE-BITES.

I'LL THROW IN A *FREE* SNAKE-BITE. C'MERE, SNAVELY.

GO AHEAD -- THINK HOW HE'LL FEEL IF YOU REFUSES.

THINK HOW I'LL FEEL IF THAT SNAKE *BITES* ME.

DOGGONE, SNAVELY! IS YOU BEEN AT THE *REMEDY* AGAIN?

HOTCHA! I BIT MYSELF, BOSS... IT WAS A CASE OF LIFE OR *WORSE.*

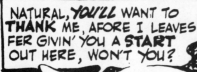

NATURAL, *YOU'LL* WANT TO **THANK** ME, AFORE I LEAVES FER GIVIN' YOU A **START** OUT HERE, WON'T YOU?

NO, BUT I'LL GIVE YOU A START *BACK*. JES' BEND OVER AN' I'LL....

HOW SHARPER THAN A CHILE'S TOOTH TO HAVE A THANKLESS SERPENT.

IF YOUSE IS RUNNIN' FOR THE *EXPRESS* IT LEFT EARLY *YESTERDAY.*

WHAT *FOR?* WE HAD SEATS *REE*SERVED.

RIGHT UNDER THE *REEFRIG-AN-ATOR* CAR.

IT **HAD** TO LEAVE YESTERDAY 'CAUSE IT'S DUE IN. **FORT MUDGE** TOMORROW.

A FIVE MILE TRIP!

I *KNOW!* BUT FORT MUDGE IS HARD TO FIND... GOIN' CROST-COUNTRY 'SPECIALLY.

WHAT TRAIN DON'T GO CROSS-COUNTRY?

WITHOUT TRACKS?

CHAPTER 17

A MOUSE TRAPS AND TRIPS

238

NOW, I WAS JUS' GOIN' LIKE THIS WHEN... ooOW...

--OWP!

YOU BULLY! PICKIN' ON THAT LI'L' SMALL WORMCHILE, THOU BEAST!

BEAST! BULLY! OGRE! BESTING A CHILE THAT WAY!

I WAS ONLY TRY AN' TO TEACH THE WORM CHILE A FEW....

A BIG STRONG MAN LIKE YOU MAKIN' A FOOL OF THAT LI'L' FELLA.... BOXIN' HIM SILLY WITH A BLINDIN' DISPLAY OF FISTIC ARTISTRY!

HE THRUN ME TWO OUT OF TWO, MIZ BEAVER, HONEST!

SSH...SH.... I KNOW....(HE WAS BEATIN' YOUR EARS OFF - SHSH..HERE'S YOUR COAT AN' STICK! THOUGHT I BETTER GIT YOU OUTEN THERE----)

(BUT IT DON'T PAY TO LET THEM OTHER MENS KNOW.) OH, THE SECRET MAGIC OF COMBAT SKILL WHAT YOU TRICKED THAT BOY WITH....! YOU BRUTE!

HEAR HER? WE MUST OF MISSED SOMETHIN'. SHE'S A EXPERT.

240

WOMAN TALKS 'BOUT EATIN'A *CHOCOLATE MOUSSE*, A MAN IN *MY* POSITION CAN'T BE *TOO* CAREFUL.

HATE TO RUN OFF FROM *MIZ BEAVER*... BUT.. *OH*.. *HEH*LO, MIZ BEAVER.

I BEEN SETTIN' HERE... CUT THRU TH' BACK WAY... HOPE TO *PER*SUADE YOU TO COME BACK..

YOU AIN'T THE CHOCOLATE MOUSSE WE HAD IN MIND ...*ALL A BIG MISTAKE*.. I BEEN PLAYIN'A GAME A·WAITIN' FOR YOU:

HE LOVE ME. *BANG!*

HE LOVE ME NOT. *BANG!*

HE LOVE ME. *BANG!*

WELL WELL WELL WELL WELL WELL WELL WELL WELL A MISTAKE EH WELL WELL WELL WELL WELL WELL WELL

WELL

WELL

WELL

WELL WELL

YOU KIN SAY *THAT* A·GAIN.

WELL WELL WELL WELL WELL WELL WELL...

WHO IS NOW AND EVER HAS BEEN A MEMBER OF THE TEA PARTY?

EVENIN', MIZ MA'M'SELLE 'HEPZIBAH..... EVENIN', MIZ BEAVER ......HEY, MOUSE.

WELCOME TO THESE *SOIRÉE*, M'SIEUR POGO.

YOU'RE JES' IN TIME FER THE REST OF MY STORY 'BOUT *FRANCE*, POGO. PULL UP A CHAIR....

THIS FELLA I RUN INTO HIS ROOM OF, TURNS OUT TO BE A BIG *PER-FUME* MAKER (*THEY PRONOUNCES IT PARAFINE*) WELL, I GIVE HIM A IDEA.. A PERFUME LIKE A BREEZE ..OPEN SPACES....FRESH AIR... FOR THE *NONCE* CALL IT "*X*".

HE IS *NATURUL DEE*LIGHTED AN' IS COUNTIN' OUT A MILLION IN *ONES* FOR ME WHEN I MENTIONS A GOOD SLOGAN: *USE "X" AND SMELL LIKE ALL OUTDOORS.* ...WELL, RIGHT THEN A VERY NASTY THING HAPPENS, HE....

HE USED TO TELL THIS'N ABOUT *LOS ANGELES* WHEN *THAT* WAS A TONEY TOWN.

OH, HOW *GAY!* THAT YEAR IN *FRANCE* WAS JUST AFORE THE *BOTTOM* FELL OUT OF THE *MARKET*. I WAS WORKIN' IN THIS FOODSTUFFS EMPORIUM ON THE *RAVIOLI* WHEN I ...

YOU MEAN ON THE *RIVIERA*, NO, M'SIEUR?

WELL, IF YOU MUST GIVE IT THE *FRENCH* PRONOUNCEMENT..*O.K.* ANYHOW, *THERE I WAS ON THIS BIG PILE OF CANNED RIVIERA*.....

THE **CAT**, WHOM IT WAS **MY** DUTY TO BE CHASED BY, CAME ALONG *SNEERIN'* IN THE MOTHER TONGUE, SO I HOLLERS OUT: *"CAMEMBERT!"* (FRENCH FOR "COME ON, BERT." THE CAT'S NAME BEIN' *BERTRAM*) WELL, SIR, THAT CAT GUV A LEAP..*WOW!*

OVER WENT THE PILE OF RIVIERA IN A **AWFUL** CRASH ..... THE FLOOR SAGGED, QUIVERED, AN' *BOOM! THE BOTTOM FELL OUT OF THE MARKET!* WE ALL LANDED IN THE CELLAR SCREAMIN' GALLICISMS WHICH BRUNG THE GENDARMES ON THE DOUBLE AN'......

HOW 'BOUT "LIZA JANE"?

STOP ME IF I'M **BORIN'** YOU BUT IT'S SUCH A CLEAR NIGHT FOR A GOOD TALK... WELL, WHEN THAT MARKET ON THE RUE DE LA CHAT COLLAPSED IT CAUSED QUITE A **STIR**...1929 IT WAS...

THE PAPERS WERE FULL OF IT.. PEOPLE SAID: *"WHY'D THE BOTTOM FALL OUT OF THE MARKET?"* HA! I **KNOW!** THE **CAT** KNOCKED OVER THE CANNED GOODS. *DID* THE EXPERTS ASK **ME?** **NO**, THEY--

THEY **MIGHT** OF BEEN THINKIN' OF ANOTHER MARKET.

Y'MEAN ANOTHER MARKET COLLAPSED THAT YEAR?

A MARKET ON *WALL STREET*.

A COINCIDENCE! WALL STREET STORE, HUH? SMALL PLACE, NO DOUBT... *NEVER HEARD OF IT*.

NO, IT HAD A LI'L' SIZE ON IT.... Y'EVER HEAR OF THIS **WALL STREET** WHAT POLITICIANS AN' **REE**VOLUTIONARY RASCALS IS ALLUS HOLLER'N' *DOWN WITH IT?*

ALWAYS THOUGHT THAT WAS A OL' *MYTHOLOGICAL* **BEAST**.... WODDYA KNOW! WELL, THIS **BIG** MARKET COLLAPSE *I* WAS IN WAS...

ALL EVENINGS IN THESE *PARTY,* MY SOIRÉE, *THESE PERSON* IS SHOOT OFF *MOUSE TRAP* AN' IS *LONG DRAW* OUT THE BOW.

HE'S *MY* GENNLEMAN GUEST! AN' IT'S AS MUCH *MY* SWARRY AS *YOURN.*

SOMETHIN' 'BOUT ME GITS WIMMEN TO FIGHTIN'.

THEY IS EASY RILED.

BUT M'SIEUR LE POGO IS HERE AWAIT WITH BANJO, WITH MUSIC, WITH SOCIETY VERSE TO PERFORM ...

SUCH AS?

ATTEND THE MENU! *SUCH AS "CASÉE A LA BATON! SUCH AS "LE BEAU PIPP!" SUCH AS "MOE LE BRANNIGAN!" THAT* IS WHAT IS SUCH AS.

MOLLY BRAN... ...*AGAIN?* US HEARN THAT *TWO YEARS RUNNIN'*!

YOU DO NO LIKE?

THAT'S *EX*ACK WHY WE WAS RUNNIN', HONEY. MOLLY OUGHT A *SUE* SOMEBODY.

ALLUS THUNK MY LOUD *BANJO* WORK COVERED MY VOICE PERTY GOOD.

WELL... YES AN' NO.

IN·AN·ASMUCH AS THE SOIRÉE IS BOGGED INTO A VERITABOBBLE *SAR-GASSO,* POGO AN' I GONE CHEER UP US.

YUP.~ PORKYPINE IS RUNNED ACROSS A NEW TUNE ..... IT GOT A LOTTA *ZIP* IN IT SO TO SPEAK ~~

I'LL ROUSE AHEAD WITH THE SOPRANO WORDS WHILST YOU FOLLY 'LONG WITH THE *BOOM A DIDDY BOOM!*

FOLLY IT IS.

♪ I S'POSE YOU HEAR OF TH' BATTLE ♫ NEW ORLEANS, ♫ WHERE OL' GEN'RAL JACKSON GIVE THE BRITISH BEANS ♫ THERE THE YANKEE BOYS DO TH' JOB SO SLICK FOR THEY COTCH OL' *PACKENHAM* AN' ROW HIM UP THE CRICK! ♫

POSSUM UP A GUM TREE.. COONY ON A *STUMP*

POSSUM UP A GUM...UH... MM..A..BOO--UH-HMM? *MY SAKES!* HOW *COULD* THEY OF RUN OFF *AFORE* THEY SEE HOW IT COME OUT?

THEY MEBBE IS ANGLO-PHILES.

MORE LIKELY MUSIC LOVERS

COME ON OUT... US IS GONE SING SOMETHIN' LESS *COUNTER-VERSIBLE*... SOMETHIN' MORE CLASSICAL...

PATER

♫ SHE HAD NO'GANE A MILE OR TWA, WHEN SHE HEARD THE *DEAD-BELL* RINGING ♫♪ ♫ AN' EVRY JOW THAT THE DEAD-BELL GEID IT CRY'D: *WOE* TO BARBARA ALLEN.

OH, MOTHER, MOTHER ♫ MAKE MY BED! ♫ ---

WELL! HAVIN'A GOOD TIME, FOLKS?

--OH, MAKE IT SAFT ♫ AN' NARROW! ♫ SINCE MY LOVE ♫ DIED FOR ME TODAY... ♫ I'LL DIE FOR *HIM* TOMORROW. ♫

SNIFF GULP! HAVIN'A MOS' WONDERFOOLS TIME..

OKAY! *OKAY!* HIT THAT "SIGHT" HARDER..... OTHER WISE, *SOLID!* Y'KNOW I WAS TALKIN' ABOUT THE *PARTY* TO OL' *TROTSKY* YESTIDDY AN' HE SAY, "THIS IS GOTTA BE **BLOWED UP** GOOD."

TROTSKY?

YEH... HIM WITH THE SIX PIECE BAND... *TURKEY TROTSKY* AND HIS *DIXIE GYPSIES* ..... HE SAY A BLUE NOTE GOTTA BE BLEW BUT *SOLID!*

OH, SURE! SOLID BLUE IS MY OWN FAVORITE SHADE.

AS WE QUIETLY TAKE **POGO'S** GRUB, (HE BEING AWAY FROM HOME LIKE THE *IRRESPONSIBLE DESPOTIC LANDLORD HE IS,*) I WORRY....

YEAH.

PENSACOLA IT'S THE SPA

I WORRY ABOUT A WORLD WHERE AN HONEST MAN NEVER KNOWS *WHO* IT IS **SAFE** TO BE **AGAINST.** ONLY YESTERDAY I TRUSTED THE TURTLE... WE'D TURNED TO HIS SIDE.... IN FACT, *JOINED 'EM!*

YEAH.

WE KNEW OF HIS **STRATIFIED STUPIDISM**...WE WERE **SURE**: *HERE WAS ONE WE COULD BE AGAINST WITH IMPLINISTIC SECURITISM!* **WHAT HAPPENS?** HE REVEALS HIS TRUE FACE ----- *HE HAS POWERFUL FRIENDS!* **WHO CAN BE TRUSTED?**

YEAH.

STOP LOOKIN' AT ME LIKE THAT.

YEAH.

A FALL CLASSIC IS FELLED

PFAH!

BOXING GLOVES! *WHO NEEDS THESE?*

M'SIEUR ALBERT IS *FOUR-FLUSHER!*

FOUR-FIVE --- YES, EVEN SIX, SEVEN OR *TWELVE FLUSHER!*

WE GONE NEED A **UMPIRE** TO PREVENT *FIGHTS.*

ROOMPH! THEY ALLUS **START** EM.

POGO IS RIGHT. *WE* NEED A *UMPIRE.*

A **ARBITER** WHO IS *TOUGH!* ONE WHO CAN BACK UP HIS OPINION... AN UMPIRE WITH **COURAGE**...WITH **STRENGTH! FEARLESS! A REAL** FIGHTER.*A REAL MAN!* WHO AMONGST US?

Oh, Miz Beaver ♪ ♫

Yoo Hoo ♪♪

HMPH! AIN'T YOU GOT NOTHIN' IN A MORE DAINTY SIZE ---'BOUT A **NINE**, *MEBBE?*

UMPIRE

HOPE YOU DON'T MIND ME *PRACTICIN'* MY **RADIO JOB,** UNCLE BALDWIN ---'TAINT HOOKED UP YET, BUT---- HERE GOES : *GOOD AFTERNOON, HERE IS A IMPORTANT PREGAME FLASH!*

SEE IT *NOW!* THE **THROBBING NEW FILM** "*CUMQUAT BLOSSOMS.*" SEE THE *ALLURIN'* **MIBSIE FARQUHAR,** THE CURVACEOUS AN' *DEE-LECTABLE* **TOO-TOO DEVINE** ---*AND* THAT SLOW BURNIN' *TIGRESS,* GREEN-EYED *FOLLY FRISBIE!*

WHY AIN'T YOU LETTIN' LI'L' *GRUN-DOON* PLAY IN YO' **WORLD SERIES** NO MORE?

IT'S *OVER*... HE **UN**RAVELED OUR **BALL.**

IF YOU AIN'T GONE LET HIM PLAY YOU OUGHT TO GIVE BACK HIM HIS BALL.

HE MADE A **HOO-RAW'S NEST** OUTEN IT.

AN' IT *WASN'T* HIS ANYHOWS... HE JES' TRY TO SWAP OFF'N HIS BIG'UN FER IT.

IF YOU AIN'T GONE LET HIM PLAY WE'LL JES' TAKE THE *BIG* ONE TOO.

I'M SORRY WE EVER LAID A *EYE* ON YO' LI'L' 'SCAPER.

IF YOU AIN'T GONE LET HIM PLAY THEY'S NO *REQUIRE* TO *APOLOGY*, MR. ALBERT. US GROUN'CHUNKS KIN TAKE A *HINT!*

CHAPTER 20

A TIGER BURNS BRIGHT

UNFORTUNATELY THIS ACCOUNT OF THE **TIGERS** AN' THE **RED BIRDS** NEVER TOLE HOW THE **CLASSIC ENDED.**

DIN'T YOU GIT THE NEXT DAY'S PAPER?

WELL, **I** **TRIED**... BUT SOMETHIN' HAPPENED TO THE **FREEDOM** OF THE **PRESS**...

WHAT!? OUR NEWSPAPERS IS BOUND BY THE RED BLOODED PRINTERS' INK WHAT COURSES THRU THEIR VEINS TO...

HEAR! HEAR!

NOT THAT... I MEAN THE **FIRST** DAY I GOT A **FREE PAPER** WHEN THE NEWSBOY IN **CHICAGO** WAS.. (*I WAS AT THE FAIR AT THE TIME*) WHEN HE WAS LOOKIN' AT A BALLOON.

BUT THE **NEXT DAY** THIS FERRET SPOTS ME AN' HE SCREAMS AFTER ME DOWN MICHIGAN BOULEVARD..... **HAH!** THE **CROWDS!** YOU'D THINK THEY NEVER SAW A TIGER SWIPE A NEWSPAPER BEFORE....

NO, I NEVER **DID** FIND OUT HOW BADLY WE BEAT THE **RED BIRDS** THAT YEAR ... FOR **ME**, FREEDOM OF THE **PRESS** ENDED WHEN...

THE **GENDARMES** INTERFERED AN' I AIN'T HAD A **FREE** PAPER SINCE ... SOMETHING ABOUT ME **ALERTS** THE MOST NUMP-BRAINED NEWSBOY... **HOWEVER**, THE TRASH BASKETS I'VE BROWSED THRU LATELY **ALL** INDICATE THE PRESS HAS **CLAMPED DOWN!**

WHERE?

WHERE?! HA?! DO WE HAVE HEADLINES LIKE *THIS* ANYMORE? MY *FAVORITE* KIND?... **NO!** THEY *BURY* THINGS!

PAPERS PRINT THE NEWS WHAT *IS*... NOT JES' WHAT YOU *WANTS,* WODDYA MEAN THEY BURY THINGS?

TIGERS WIN 1934 FLAG

HERE'S A PAPER (WRAPPED 'ROUND A FISH) AUG. 29 1953. *BURY THINGS?!* LOOK WHERE THEY PUT **DE**TROIT IN THE STANDIN'S.. *SEVENTH PLACE!* 40 GAMES BURIED! THAT DIDN'T HAPPEN IN *MY* DAY, FRIENDS!

IT'S *MY* CONTENTION, FRIENDS, IF WE HAD A *TRULY* LIBERAL PRESS THE **TIGERS** WOULD OF GOT A BETTER SPOT IN THE *AMERICAN LEAGUE STANDINGS*... SUCH THINGS ARE NOT THE WHIM OF CHANCE....

THEY IS THE WHIM OF WHAMMY.

OL' ROY MATSON

FORGET SPORTS ...*TAKE THEM COMICKAL* STRIPS ...A NEWS PAPER BUYS A STRIP AN' WILL IT LET OTHER PAPERS IN THE SAME TOWN HAVE IT, TOO?

HA! TALK ABOUT FREEDOM.

ROY MATSON

BESIDES.... **WHO..** *WHAT* PITIFUL PIT- TANCE READS THE PAPERS TODAY?

WELL, THERE'S A WAY OVER 50,000,000 COPIES EVER'DAY READ BY, AT THE VERY LEAST, TWO PEOPLE APIECE.

WELL, YOU DON'T HAVE TO **SNAP** MY HEAD OFF.

DIN'T KNOW IT WAS MADE OF RUBBER, SON.

HUMPH!

LAST TIME A PAPER MENTIONED ME THEY SPELT MY NAME WRONG.

SEE, YOU IS FUSSIN' 'BOUT A FREE PRESS AN' THE MINUTE THEY MAKES **FREE** WITH YO' NAME, YOU GITS **MAD.**

CRITTURS IS **ALL** ALIKE.

WHAT MAKES YOU SO TALKY? THEM'S THE **FIRST** WORDS YOU SAID SINCE **WENSDAY.**

I BEEN MULLIN' AT 'EM.

NEWSPAPERS ARE PUT OUT BY CRITTURS JES' LIKE OTHER THINGS IS DID BY CRITTURS... SOMETIMES GOOD... SOMETIMES NOT SO... BUT CONSIDERIN' THAT EVER'BODY IS GOT TWO LEFT FEET US CRITTURS DON'T DO BAD...

I FIGGERS, PORKY, THAT **EVERY MAN'S HEART IS EVENTUAL** IN THE **RIGHT PLACE.**

AN' **I** FIGGERS POGO, THAT IF A MAN'S GONNA BE **WRONG** 'BOUT SOMETHIN', **THAT** IS THE **BEST** WRONG THING TO KEEP BEIN' WRONG ABOUT, 'TIL **FOREVER.**

CHAPTER 21

AN EPISODE
THAT GOES OFF HALF COCKNEY

I S'Y, ALF, IF IT AIN'T ONE OF THEM, NOW, 'EDGEHOG CHAPS.

RIGHTO, REGGIE... 'EY GUV'NOR, WHICH WAY TO THE *CRICKET MATCH*?

COR! 'E'S COLD GRAVY, ALF; *E* NEVER 'EARD OF THE GYME, BY THE LOOK OF 'IM.

THE ROUNDER SERIES FOR THE WORLD CUP, Y'KNOW!'

ALF, LAD, IF YOU TYKE NOTE, *E'S* WEARIN' A GRASS **KILT**. *LUMME!* S'POSE 'E'S A *HAWAIIAN*?

IF 'E *IS*... 'E'S A *LYDY*... AN' ME WITH ME *TOPPER* ON.

COO! 'E'S NO HAWAIIAN... WHERE'S HIS *GUITAR* AN' 'IS BLINKIN' *PINE-APPLE*?

(AS I S'Y, REGGIE, 'E'S A *FÉMYLE*... THEY DON'T CARRY THEM) *A THOUSAND PARDONS*, MADAM.

THINK I'LL GO BACK.... 'LONG AS HE SAID WHAT HE SAID ....

ONE OF YOU IS SAID TO ME..."*A THOUSAN' PARDONS, MADAM.*" SO... HOW ABOUT 'EM?

BLINK ME EYE, IF SHE AIN'T A TALKER AT THAT, REGGIE...... *RIGHTO*, MA'M. WHAT ABOUT 'EM AS *YOU* SAYS, MADAM?

264

CHAPTER 22

A SCANDAL FOR SCHOOL

OL' **OWL** GONE OPEN UP A **SCHOOL**, HOUN' DOG.

GREAT NEWS! YES, **INDEED**.

MY SCHOOL DAYS ... THE GOLDEN YEARS IN FIRST GRADE WERE GONE TOO SOON ... I'VE OFT WONDERED WHAT HAPPENED TO OUR MANUAL TRAININ' TEACHER AN' FOOTBALL COACH ..

A GREAT GUY, HUH?

A LADY ... MISS **BOOMBAH** - WE LOVED HER LIKE A BROTHER ... CALLED HER "*SIS*" ... WE HAD A CHEER FOR SPORTING CONTESTS .... *YAY WILLACOOCHIE! GLORIOUS WILLACOOCHIE EVER TRUE! FIGHT ON, CHARTROOS AN' PLAID!*

WILLACOO-*CHEEE! SIS BOOMBAH.'*" WE **ALWAYS** TACKED **HER** ON THE **END**. SHE HOLLERED LOUDER'N ANYBODY ...

I SHOULDA THUNK SHE WOULD

THIS NOW, *SCHOOL* .... SOON'S I GIT ANOTHER **BENCH** MADE IT'S GONE BE A *SURE 'NUFF* **U**-NIVERSITY ...

GOOD FOR *IT.'*

I'LL HELP YOU TEACH ALL 'BOUT MY **SPECIALTY** .... BECAUSE I IS A **EXPERT** ON MY SPECIALTY .... AN' IS A **SPECIALIST** ON IT TOO BESIDES.

YOUR STUDENT BODY IS *PREE-* PARED TO GIVE YOU *TEMPORARY UNDERPINNIN'*, PROF.

THEN YOU KIN GIT OVER TO YOUR AUNTIE'S...... *MIZ MYRTLE* IS BOUND TO REMEMBER HOW TO GIT YO' *LEG BONES OUTEN* YO' SHELL ..... *EASY NOW*....

GOT HIM...

OKAY... NORTH BY NORTH EAST- EAST BY WEST- SOUTH-WEST MEN... *BRISK!*

PHOO...MOST DANGEROUS THING I COULD GET WOULD BE *MORE* HELP LIKE *THAT.*

GOOD NEWS, OWL! *GOOD NEWS!* WE IS COMIN' OVER TO *JOIN YOUR FACULTY!*

WHOOOP! KEERFUL.

IS YOU FOLKS COMIN' TO *SCHOOL?*

YES, *YES!* WE'RE *ACHIN'* TO START...

WHERE'S THE *STADIUM?* WE GOT THE *BACKFIELD* ALL FIGGERED OUT....

NO SPORTS ALLOWED!

271

CHAPTER 23

A FORM OF HIRE EDUCATION

IF YOU IS MAKIN' A **SURVEY** ON US **MAIL MENS** YOU OUGHTTA **ACCEPT** THE ANSWERS WE GIVES.

BUT THE ANSWERS YOU GIVE ARE *COLORLESS* AND DO **NOT** FIT OUR THEORETICAL PATTERN.

FOR EXAMPLE WHEN I ASK IF YOU PREFER **PURPLE** TO **BLUE** ON THE **FOUR** CENT STAMP OR ON THE **FIVE**, *YOU DON'T ANSWER WITH A SIMPLE YES OR NO.*

OK. PUT ME DOWN FOR A SIMPLE "MAYBE."

FURTHER, WHY DO YOU NOT WEAR **SNOWSHOES**? DO YOU HAVE A DEEP ROOTED DESIRE TO IGNORE WINTER?

NO, THEY LETS THE COLD THRU ON MY TOEBONES AN' BESIDES IT'S **ONLY** NOVEMBER.

WHY DO YOU HATE POOR **NOVEMBER**? WHY BELITTLE IT, SAYING "*ONLY*"?

DAG NAB IT! I WISHT YOU'D LET ME DELIVER THIS **SPECIAL** --- IT'S FOR **ME** AN' I CAN'T WAIT TO GIT HOME SO I'LL BE THERE WHEN IT COMES.

DO YOU MEAN TO SAY YOU'RE **BREAKING OFF** THE INTERVIEW?

I GOTTA **GO**! IF I'M OUT HERE I CAN'T BE **HOME** AN' CAN'T GET THE **LETTER** I GOT TO DELIVER TO ME.

BUT IF YOU'RE AT HOME YOU CAN'T BE **ON DUTY** AN' IF YOU'RE NOT **ON** YOU CAN'T **DELIVER** THE MAIL.

I DON'T CARE! I DON'T CARE! I DON'T CARE AN' ANYWAY I CAN SO.

I DO DECLARE, POGO, IT'S EXTREMELY DIFFICULT FOR AN ELDERLY BACHELOR GIRL TO MAKE A LIVING; SO I TOOK A JOB WITH DR. *WHIMSEY*...

BY *JING!* MY OL' FOOTBALL COACH, *SIS BOOMBAH*, UP IN *PROVIDENCE*, ALLUS SAID ROADWORK IS MIGHTY BENEFICIAL...

'SPECIALLY IF YOU IS ON THE LAM...

BOOP!

HAVE A CARE, SON, I'M AN *OLD LADY*... ...SO, AS I SAY, POGO, I'M HELPING DR. WHIMSEY AND...

MISS BOOMBAH!

WHO MIGHT *YOU* BE, PRAY TELL, WHO?

GEE, MISS *BOOMBAH*, DON'T YOU RECOGNIZE AN OLD *STUDENT* FROM UP IN *PROVIDENCE*?

YOU'RE THAT OLD *TROUBLE MAKER* LITTLE ROBBIE HALL...

OW! I AM *NOT!*

NOTHING TAUGHT HERE

FEARLESSLY

QUICK! QUICK!

THE TEAM IS AT PRACTICE.

CAPTAIN C GLENN ADLOX

HOT DOG! I DON'T WANT TO MISS THIS! WAIT FOR ME!

YOU'RE JUST IN TIME.

I'M ALL TUNED UP... WHERE'S THE REST OF THE TEAM?

RIGHT OVER THERE, YOUNG MAN, GET THE BEANBAG, PLEASE.

BEAN BAG!? AND A TEAM OF BIRDS! HOW CAN WE EVER FACE U.C.L.A.?

OH, THE BIRDS ARE NOT ON THE SQUAD. I HIT BEAUREGARD WITH A LOOSE SACK OF WHITE NAVIES AN' NOW HE'S ALIVE WITH COMMON GRACKLES.

I'LL BRUSH THE BIRDS AN' BEANS OFF, HOUN'DOG, AN' MEBBE YOU'LL EXPLAIN.

WELL, SIS BOOMBAH OFFERED TO COACH THE TEAM ON ACCOUNT SHE COACHED MY FIRST GRADE TO THE CHAM-PEENSHIP FIVE YEAR STRAIGHT!

POOT

BUT HOW COME YOU IS COVERED WITH BEANS? WHAT WILL NOTER DAME SAY WHEN WE SHOWS UP PLAYIN' BEAN-BAG!?

282

284

PSST~PORKY..... WHILE WE'RE IN A HUDDLE---HERE'S A *T.V. ROUSER*: YOU ALWAYS KNOW WHAT GAL IS ON *T.V.*....

ALL SET, MEN?! GOT THEM SIGNALS?

THEN, *HIKE!* LINE UP!

'CAUSE YOU CAN ALWAYS TELE-VISION GIRL~*HA!* RICH, EH? HO HO?

LET'S GO! LET'S GO!

Pardon, Porky. What did he say?

TOLE A VERY FUNNY STORY: YOU CAN ALLUS TELL A *TEEVY* GAL 'CAUSE SHE'S ON T.V.

Hmm~~~What can you tell her? That's the point!

BUT YOU CAN'T TELL HER MUCH, MAYBE.....

---A CRYPTICISM OF HUMOR----A VERY VERY DANGEROUS WEAPON.

THE MYSTERIOUS HUDDLES THE MEN CONDUCT *BEHIND THE LINES*----HMP! PRETTY SUSPICIOUS.

As a committee of parents, we'll see the President of this new college and find out what he's teaching

BUT *WE* AIN'T PARENTS..

So much more credit we deserve for our unselfish concern, then.

Owl, this committee demands to know what you've been teaching.

NOTHIN'! NOT A THING— I BEEN SO BUSY SIGNIN' THESE DIPLOMAS I AIN'T HAD NO TIME TO TEACH 'EM NOTHIN'!

Nothing, eh? If you're teaching them nothing they can't learn much— That's perfectly all right, isn't it, men?

NOT SO FAST. WHAT KINDA NOTHIN'?

YOU SAID, OWL, THAT YOUR COLLEGE WAS TEACHIN' 'EM NOTHIN'; WHAT KIND OF NOTHIN'?

I'M STANDIN' UP FER ACADEMIC FREEDOMS! I'LL TEACH NOTHIN' AS I PLEASES.

YOU HEARD HIM.... WHO KNOWS WHAT KIND OF NOTHIN' HE WILL TEACH? HE MAY BE AN ADVOCATE OF ANONYMOUS ANIMOSITISM!

TAKE IT FROM US EXPERTS. WE BEEN THRU IT.

Professor Owl, do you mean you'd even teach 'em nothing about Alien Ideologics?

ANYTHIN' I HAPPEN TO KNOW NOTHIN' 'BOUT, I'LL TEACH IT IF I GOT THE STREN'TH!

This is a new approach— Controlled Ignorance— we must give this thought.

ACADEMIC FREEDOMS, MY EYE!

SIR, MY FREEDOMS IS AS ACADEMIC AS THEY COME.

WHO REALLY
INVENTED NOTHING?

WHILST THE *BEAN BAG* SCRIMMAGE IS GOIN' ON, I COME TO ASK KIN I CARRY YO' BOOKS TO SCHOOL, MIZ MA'M'SELLE HEPZIBAH...

BUT I AM NOT GO, M'SIEUR...

THUNK YOU'D TEACH *FRENCH*----*EVER'- BODY ELSE IS GONE TEACH*---'CEPT *ME.* I BRUNG YOU A COUPLE APPLES IN CASE YOU *WAS* ...

BUT, NOW I ARE NOT--- ---SO *NO FRUIT?* NO?

NAW...NO HARD FEELIN'S.....GUESS I'LL TEACH IT MYSELF. SO I'LL HELP YOU EAT YO' APPLES WHILST I THINKS UP SOME FRENCH TO TEACH.

BUT YOU DO NO MAKE UP THE FRENCH. IT IS *ALL* READY TO *GO*----ALL IS TO DO IS HEAT HIM AN' SERVE.

WHAT!? I ALLUS THOUGHT YOU WAS JES' MESSIN' AROUN' INVENTIN' THAT *FRENCH* OUTEN YO' OWN LI'L' HEAD.....SO *YOU* REALLY *DIN'T* MAKE IT ALL UP, HUH?

NO, ALAS, IF I OWN THE COPYRIGHT OF FRENCH I WOULD BE VER' *HEALTHEE* FELLOW.

GREAT *NEWS*, FELLOWS! I HAVE BOOKED A GAME WITH **IGLOO U.** FROM UP IN THE *TUNDRA.*

GREAT! NEXT STOP: THE *ROSE BOWL!*

FIRST WE MUST CONQUER CALIFORNIA!

AAH---WE'LL TAKE 'EM *EASY!*

HEAR THAT?

WE HEARD WHAT THEY'RE PLOTTIN' IN THEM HUDDLES. *REVOLUTION!* ANARCHY!

THEY'RE GONNA STEAL CALIFORNIA!

'Incredible'

PHOO..WHUFFO AN' BESIDES WHERE WOULD THEY *KEEP* IT?

LET'S GO, EVER'BODY, FOR A RIDE IN THE NEW BOAT WE NAMED FOR DOCTOR CARL.

STOP BEIN' SO *BROODY*, DEACON. C'MON.

What? With these students plotting to steal California....?

BUT, AS M'SIEUR *PORK* LE *PINE* IS SAY: *WHERE ARE THESE CAULIFORN TO BE KEPT IF HE IS STOLING?*

DOC CARL HARTMAN

Phaugh! They'll keep it in Florida perchance or sell it in South America ----- The whole idea fills me with *Loathing*

I FEEL THE *SAME!*

YES SIR!

If you two feel like I do -- *How* can you both look so happy?

WE'RE *ALWAYS HAPPY* WHEN WE'RE FILLED WITH *LOATHING.*

SURE.. AIN'T *YOU?*

THE HON. FRED W. GIESEL

CHAPTER 26

THE CAROLS GROUND OUT...
FIRST BASS TO SHORT

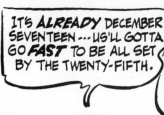

IT'S *ALREADY* DECEMBER SEVENTEEN...US'LL GOTTA GO *FAST* TO BE ALL SET BY THE TWENTY-FIFTH.

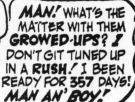

MAN! WHAT'S THE MATTER WITH THEM *GROWED-UPS?* I DON'T GIT TUNED UP IN A *RUSH!* I BEEN READY FOR 357 DAYS! *MAN AN' BOY!*

GMX.

QUIET, YOU TADS. ALL RIGHT, NOW, FIRST: "*HERE WE GO A-WAFFLIN'.*" HIT IT!

WURF.

WANG A BLANG WAM A SOCK

WODDYA THINK OF *THAT* ONE, CHURCHY?

HARD FOR ME TO SAY-- I THINK I'M *TOO CLOSE* TO IT---

HOW 'BOUT US PLAYIN' *HOOKEY* FROM CAROL PRACTICE AN' GOIN' ON A *EXPEDITION?*

YOU BOTH KNOWS THE WORDS TO THE "*TWELVE DAYS OF CHRISTMAS*" AN' ALL?

GBNX.

WURF WURF.

I **THOUGHT** SO... MAM SAYS **CHILLUNS** IS THE SINGLE TYPE CRITTURS WHAT IS **ALWAYS** PREE-PARED FOR CHRISTMAS... IF CHRISTMAS WAS **DECLARED** ON **FOURTH OF JULY**... **US** WOULD BE **READY!**

GROWED FOLKS IS THE **ONLY** ONES WHAT GOTTA PRACTICE UP GITTIN' IN THE **MOOD**... SPRING **DEC. 25** ON 'EM SUDDEN AN' **HALF** WOULDN'T HAND OUT THEIR **RIGHT NAMES**.

WHY ISN'T YOU TADS PRACTICIN' UP FOR CHRISTMAS LIKE ALL THE OTHERS?

SHUCKS, US CHILLUN IS BEEN READY **ALL** THE **WHOLE YEAR**.

READY FOR WHAT EVER COMES, HUH? Y'ALL KIN **SPELL** YO' NAME GOOD SO'S WHEN YOU SEES A PACKAGE TAGGED FOR **YOU** YOU'LL OPEN IT RIGHT QUICK...

YOU BETCHA!

AN' ALL YEAR YOU SHOWED YO' MAMS AN' PAPS, YO' UNCLES, AUNTS AN' KIN THAT THE WORLD IS REALLY A PLACE OF LOVE BY BEIN' SWEET TO 'EM... KEEPIN' 'EM AS READY FOR CHRISTMAS AS YOU IS? HELPIN' 'EM GIT THROUGH?

WELL----

WELL... THINK THERE'S STILL TIME TO GIVE 'EM A HAND THAT WAY, UNCLE PORKY?

AW... THERE'S **ALLUS** TIME FOR IT PROVIDIN' YOU DON'T WASTE NONE OF IT.

UNCLE PORKY'S *RIGHT!* IT'S ONLY *FAIR* FOR US TADS TO HELP OUR *MAMS* AN' *PAPS* INTO THE *PROPER CHRISTMAS MOOD!*

CAROL NUMBER THREE NOW... *EVERYBODY QUIET...* ONE TWO A THREE...

HEY MA!

DECK US ALL WITH *BOSTON CHARLIE, WALLA WALLA WASH., AN' KALAMAZOO!* NORA'S FREEZIN' ON THE *TROLLEY SWALLER DOLLAR CAULIFLOWER ALLEY-GA-ROO!*

THAT WAS FOR *NOTHIN'...* SO WATCH OUT.

WHILST CHURCHY IS LOOKIN' UP A NEW CAROL, US KIN *REE*-LAX WITH A LI'L' SNACK.

GOOD MOR-ROW, KIND SIRS...WE IS LI'L' *WASS'LERS,* WASS'LIN' LIKE GOOD FELLAS... US WASSAILS WHILE YOU WAITS.

NO NO... WE IS THE WAITS.

RIGHT HE IS ... WE IS LI'L' *ENGLISH WAITS* ... WOULDST WE WHISTLE UP A WASSAIL, WENCESLAS?

BACK OFF'N THE LUNCH!

NOW, ALBERT.

JA, MEIN STADT-HOLDER. LET'S US WASSAIL 'EM TO A FALL.

FREE STYLE.

AN' SO ALL TO BED——————

DUNNO **WHY** I BOTHER WITH THIS YEAR AFTER YEAR... **HALLOO!** WAKE UP! **CHRISTMAS EVE!**

OH... IT'S **YOU**, PORKY... DON'T YOU KNOW YOU AN' ME IS FILLED THE STOCKIN'S AN' JES' FINISH TRIMMIN' THE **TREES? IT'S FOUR A.M.**

SO.....YOU DON'T **NEED** A WATCH?

THAT'S GOOD, 'CAUSE HERE'S SOMETHIN' I BEEN SAVIN' FOR YOU SINCE **AUGUST**... NOW, PLEASE, DON'T **FAWN** ON ME.....**A SPRIG** OF **LOVE-IN-IDLENESS** ---'TAIN'T MUCH, **BUT,** THE WAY FOLKS TREATS EACH OTHER NOW-A-DAYS.....

..IF I LEAVES THIS UP TO **ANY BODY ELSE, YOU'LL** BE LUCKY IF YOU RECEIVES A **SIMPLE GOOD MORNIN'!**

AW... YOU OL' **PORKYPINE**...**I DO** B'LEEVE I'LL WAKE UP AN' MAKE COCOA AN' **PEANER BUTTER SAN'WICHES.**

CHAPTER 27

ONE FINAL WORD
LEADS TO ANOTHER

THIS NEW MAN YOU IS GONE BE.... *WHO IS HE?* WHO YOU GONE BE?

OH... MEBBE I'LL BE **PRESIDENT GRANT**... I HEAR HE GOT A BIG PLACE UP ON **RIVERSIDE DRIVE**... RENT FREE!

NO... THAT JOB IS BEEN DONE... YOU GOTTA BE A *BRAN'NEW* SOMEBODY.

WODDYA MEAN THE JOB'S **DONE**? *THERE'S STILL A DEE*·MAND.... **STILL ROOM** AT THE TOP, MY FRIEND.

YOU WON'T LIKE BEIN' UP ON THAT DRIVE... TOO MANY CARS... TOO MUCH **TRAFFIC**...

THEN I COULD SET UP AS A *TRAFFIC COP.* THINK OF THE BUSINESS I'D GET!

YOU'D GET THE BUSINESS AN' YOU'D **DESERVE** IT··· UH, HOW CAN YOU TEAR YOURSELF AWAY, POGO?

YOU GOT A REASON TO LEAVE?

NO···· BUT I'LL THINK OF SOMETHIN'

CHURCHY BEEN TALKIN' TO **BUN RABBIT**... CLAIMIN' HE'S GONE BE A NEW MAN BUT CAN'T FIGGER WHO...

HERE HE COME... HE LOOK JES' LIKE **LAST YEAR** AN' EVEN MORE LIKE THE ONE AFORE THAT.

DID YOU AN' OL' BUN DECIDE WHO YOU'S TO BE FOR THE NEW YEAR?

I TURNED HIM OFF WITH A **OLD JEST**... TOLE HIM I IS GONE BE A *APPLE SELLER* SEEIN'AS IT MOUGHT BE A RAGE.

I SAID I'LL SELL **FIVE CENT** APPLES FOR *FOUR CENTS*. HE SAYS BUT YOU'LL LOSE MONEY... AN' I SAYS YES, BUT THINK OF THE TURN OVER...

WHAT TURNOVER?

THE **APPLE** TURNOVER.

OH, WELL, WHY DON'T YOU SELL **COFFEE**, TOO? THERE'S *NAUGHT* LIKE A CUP OF GOOD HOT COFFEE AN' A WARM TURNOVER ON A COLD DAY...

AN' IT **IS** GITTIN' COLDER, AIN'T IT?

DOES YOU *EVER* KNOW WHAT YOU IS TALKIN' 'BOUT?

NOPE-- AN' THAT MAKES ME **EVEN** WITH MOST FOLKS.

H'LO, **MR. WEEVIL**, OUR **COLLEGE TEAM** IS PLAYIN' *IGLOO U.*, COME FRIDAY IN A **BIG BOWL GAME.**

WELL, *BOOLA BOO-LAH* FOR **YOU**, SIR.

B WEEVIL
BOWLS
POLES
MEALS
SOALS

I COME TO SEE IS YOU GOT A LARGE CAPACITY BOWL.

NOT *HAIRCUT* SIZE, HUH....MORE **LARGE FAMILY SIZE**...SOMETHIN' WHAT'LL HOLD QUITE A NUMBER?

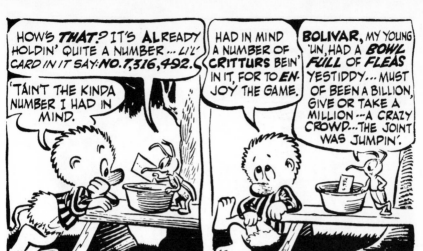

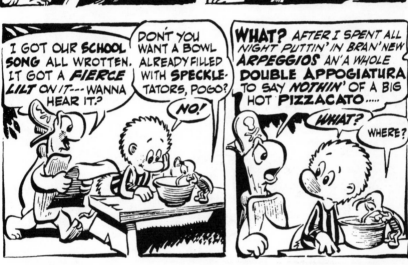

THE ESTATE OF OUR INDEPENDENCE

Sculling alertly through the waters of a Sunday afternoon we listen to the radio reports, hurried to our anxious ears through the driving rain, reports of drownings, highway accidents, death by design, explosions of small boys. When the clamor has died and is replaced by the soothing strains of George M. Cohan played upon organ and drum, the soft voice of man's best friend, his wife, observes: "Holiday rain. All those people died for nothing. . . . At least they might have had better weather for it."

And indeed they might have. In fact, we might all have better weather as we jostle toward the finish. Too soon we breast the tape and too late we realize the fun lay in the running. We deny that the end justifies the means without ever stopping to consider that for practical purposes the End and the Means are one and the same thing. If there is to be any satisfaction in life it must come in transit, for who can tell when he will be struck down in mid-method?

So, as we speed along, running up our colors and running down our neighbors, it might be well to avoid being hoist by our own halyards. In this Era of the Boomerang it is easy to counter suspicion with suspicion. It is not quite as easy to return hate for love but many of us manage it through the simple procedure of viewing all love with the suspicion reserved for the unknown. This is unfortunate because love takes many forms (not all of them immediately identifiable and therefore even more suspect). One of these forms is humor.

Naturally the humorist in any age is viewed with some misgivings for he plays with no particular team. He performs the duties of a busy-body umpire who may be expected to hit, run, field the ball and call himself out on a close play at home. The fact that he may work equally well and equally often for all teams does not make him any more dependable. He is not to be trusted.

These very thoughts are highly suspicious because it has long been the cheerful habit of nearly every American to think fondly of himself as a humorist. And, with his flair for irreverence, his social impudence, his unblinking recognition of the truth, the American, by and large over the centuries, has been a humorous man.

Currently we have narrowed our formula for the joke down to a safe channel alive with harbor lights, bell buoys, constant soundings from the bow, shouted warnings from the shore, signal fires and manned life-boats. Such channeled activity can become ritual.

A form of ritualistic humor crept into the habits and ceremonies of the ancient North American Indians. These Original Americans employed at least one comic device (a sure-fire boff) that consisted of several humorists smearing and throwing dung over some selected colleague.

As humor, the act had one serious drawback in that it became impossible, eventually, to embrace the target in a show of good fellowship directly after the performance.

Another Original American is named by a less original American as the authority on Vigilantics who taught that a suspicious man should kick rapidly upon the groin of a suspect until the latter is made helpless. This provides mirth for spectator and raconteur.

All of this good fun, the smearing, the throwing, the kicking, is spoiled when the scape-goat is not a good sport. It is one of the major requirements of joke-function that the butt should either (A) be quiet or (B) get lost . . . if he is not already rendered dead.

The Era of the Boomerang is putting our national sense of humor to a severe test. The full import of inventing the world's most devastating weapon was not realized until we learned that the enemy, acting like cads, had swiped the secret. Having been prepared to snigger, we are not prepared to applaud; but neither should we be ready to whimper.

It is not the time for a man to demonstrate the strength of his guts with a belly-laugh, but nevertheless here is a comic situation. It is a comedy in the classic tradition, so near to tragedy that the difference is indiscernible to the participant. This classic comedy is fundamentally that of the Pompous Ass falling on his bulging behind. It is nearly always funny to the onlooker. It is seldom funny to the Pompous Ass. Like it or not, however, the joke remains . . . and it is on us.

So, as we move along, we cannot care who sings our country's songs; beneath the high notes of patriotism, we want to hear the low notes of laughter, always off-key, always true.

Jagged, imperfect and lovely, the goal lies here. This is the estate of our independence.

WALT KELLY